Organize Your

Office

...In No Time

A
B
C

Monica Ricci

que®

800 East 96th Street
Indianapolis, Indiana 46240

Organize Your Office In No Time

International Standard Book Number: 0-7897-3218-1

Library of Congress Catalog Card Number: 2004117482

Printed in the United States of America

First Printing: July 2005

08   07   06   05   4   3   2   1

Trademarks

Warning and Disclaimer

Bulk Sales

Que Publishing offers excellent discounts on this book when ordered in quantity for bulk purchases or special sales. For more information, please contact

U.S. Corporate and Government Sales
1-800-382-3419
corpsales@pearsontechgroup.com

For sales outside of the U.S., please contact

International Sales
international@pearsoned.com

Executive Editor
Candace Hall

Development Editor
Lorna Gentry

Managing Editor
Charlotte Clapp

Project Editor
Seth Kerney

Production Editor
Heather Wilkins

Indexer
Aaron Black

Technical Editor
Susan Kousek

Publishing Coordinator
Cindy Teeters

Interior Designer
Anne Jones

Cover Designer
Anne Jones

Cover Illustrator
Nathan Clement, StickMan Studio

Page Layout
Michelle Mitchell

Contents at a Glance

Table of Contents

II Organizing Your Files

III Organizing Your Workspace

V Appendix

About the Author

Monica Ricci has been an organizing and productivity expert since 1998. She helps her clients by teaching them how to de-clutter, prioritize, streamline, and organize their lives both at home and at work. She is a regular expert organizer on the popular Home and Garden Television program, *Mission: Organization*. As a motivational speaker, Monica presents seminars and keynotes on time management, overcoming procrastination, getting organized, and the power of living a simpler life. Monica's business philosophy is to teach people new skills, help them think in new ways, and inspire them to change their lives for the better. She holds the core belief that when you teach people new skills, help them clarify their priorities and inspire them to action, they can dramatically transform their lives.

Monica is very active in the National Association of Professional Organizers (NAPO), having served two terms as the President of NAPO Georgia and is serving on several NAPO committees at the national level. A respected member of her industry, Monica was chosen to host a discussion panel at the National Association of Professional Organizers national conferences in 2003, 2004, and 2005. She also moderates two popular Internet forums and teaches national teleclasses. Monica writes articles, many of which have been published both locally and nationally. She lives in Atlanta, Georgia with her husband, Ed King, and their two cats.

Dedication

To my husband, Ed King; my late mother, Joan Kuhn Gutshall; and my late grandparents, Rachel Magaro Kuhn and Stanley Kuhn, whose influence in my life has been profound.

Acknowledgments

To my wonderful husband, Ed King, whom I love, respect, and admire. Your character, kind heart, and creative spirit continue to inspire me. I am blessed and honored by your commitment to my growth. You are my champion.

To each member of my family; thank you for believing in me and celebrating my successes.

To my closest and dearest friends—you know who you are. Your love, support, and encouragement enrich my life tremendously.

To all my clients over the years, who have taught me the value of flexibility, compassion, patience, empathy, and gratitude. I am humbled by your trust.

To the National Association of Professional Organizers who continues to offer me education, camaraderie, opportunities for leadership, and a vision for the future of Professional Organizing. Thank you.

To my esteemed colleagues, Judith Kolberg, Betsy Wilkowsky, Shawn Kershaw, Dorothy Breininger, and Barry Izsak. Your friendship, support, and confidence mean the world to me.

To the other organizing authors of the Que *In No Time* series; Barry Izsak, K.J. McCorry, Val Sgro, and Debbie Stanley. Your insight, humor, and encouragement is invaluable.

To Candy Hall, Lorna Gentry, and the rest of the amazing Que Publishing team; your encouragement, feedback, and patient guidance was key to the success of this project. Thank you!

We Want to Hear from You!

As the reader of this book, *you* are our most important critic and commentator. We value your opinion and want to know what we're doing right, what we could do better, what areas you'd like to see us publish in, and any other words of wisdom you're willing to pass our way.

As an executive editor for Que Publishing, I welcome your comments. You can email or write me directly to let me know what you did or didn't like about this book—as well as what we can do to make our books better.

Please note that I cannot help you with technical problems related to the topic of this book. We do have a User Services group, however, where I will forward specific technical questions related to the book.

When you write, please be sure to include this book's title and author as well as your name, email address, and phone number. I will carefully review your comments and share them with the author and editors who worked on the book.

Email: feedback@quepublishing.com

Mail: Candace Hall
         Executive Editor
         Que Publishing
         800 East 96th Street
         Indianapolis, IN 46240 USA

For more information about this book or another Que Publishing title, visit our website at www.quepublishing.com. Type the ISBN (excluding hyphens) or the title of a book in the Search field to find the page you're looking for.

Introduction

Whether you work in a plush, high-rise corner office, in a cube, or out of your home, chances are you spend a great deal of your life in your office. Creating a work environment that fosters productivity is important. If you find yourself overwhelmed, procrastinating, mired in paperwork, ineffective, unproductive, and not nearly as successful as you know you could be, office chaos has taken over. You're not alone, however. Many business people complain of feeling the same way you do and disorganization is a common challenge that crosses all boundaries.

What *Organize Your Office In No Time* Can Do For You

The *In No Time* series of books is designed to help you tackle any challenging task, using a step-by-step approach to accomplishing your goal. I've written this book in a straight-forward, simple style, and I've included plenty of photos, illustrations, and specific recommendations so you can move through the process of organizing your office quickly and efficiently. *Organize Your Office In No Time* will help you determine what kind of office organization will work best for you, how to quickly customize your office to match that organization, and how to keep it organized without sacrificing your day to maintenance. You'll get simple, practical solutions without being told that there is one "right" way to organize your office. And I offer you several organizational options, so you can choose the ones that best fit your personality and work style.

This book will teach you

- How to identify your own organizing and working style
- How to choose the organizing methods that work best for you
- How to take the overwhelming feelings out of organizing your office by approaching the task in small, manageable chunks
- Fundamental concepts and organizing principles you can apply in other areas of your life
- Techniques to help you make faster decisions to keep your office organized
- How to maximize the storage space in your office
- Simple maintenance routines to keep your office organized

Who Should Read This Book

Many people say, "I wasn't born an organizer", which might be true, but you weren't born knowing how to walk, either. Like walking or any other skill, the ability to organize is something you can learn. And like any other skill, parts of it will come easily to you and some other parts might not, but in the end, you will have learned something new and valuable. This book is for you if

- Your office environment is so chaotic you just can't focus on your work.
- You frequently miss meetings, lose important information, or find yourself re-creating the same documents over and over again.
- You know you could be so much more effective if you were more organized.
- You have lost a job or a promotion because of your lack of organizational skills.
- Your disorganization has eroded your self-confidence.
- Your disorganization is causing problems in your relationships with your boss or colleagues.
- You are busy and you think you don't have the time to get organized.

You might already be effective and productive at work and have organizational systems in place that work for you, which is terrific! Even if that's the case, however, chances are you have a few areas where you know you could improve and you just need some ideas to get you there. If so, this is the right book for you, too.

How This Book Is Organized

To help you quickly find the areas you need most, *Organize Your Office In No Time* is divided into four main parts.

Part I, "Getting Started," is a 30,000-foot view of your organizing project. Taking this big-picture, overview approach in the beginning will help you create a plan to work from that will ultimately result in your creating the office you desire. You'll learn your primary work style, decide your goals for your office space, learn how to create the framework for the space, and some time management tips to increase your effectiveness.

Part II, "Organizing Your Files," teaches you how to store, retrieve, and manage information—both paper and electronic—to keep you organized and in control. This section will also give you a range of filing system ideas and product reviews that will not only give you a jump start before you purchase, but will reduce your research time considerably.

Part III, "Organizing Your Desk," explores many viable options for organizing your desk, computer, and email; managing your contacts; and staying organized when traveling. You'll be amazed at how easy it is to use technology to become and remain organized.

Part IV, "Simple Storage Solutions," delves into helping you find the overlooked but useful storage spaces in your office, such as the vertical space on walls, doors, and furniture. You will also learn how to make effective use of offsite storage facilities for archival records and nonessential items and information.

How to Use This Book

This book won't take you long to read and you should feel welcome to skip around to the chapters that interest you most. It is designed so you can use the table of contents to pinpoint the areas you are most interested in learning about. I do recommended that you read Part I so you can have a starting point to create your organizing plan. However, if all you need are tips on filing or email management, you can certainly single out those sections to read first so you can get right to work and see results quickly. In addition, each chapter in Parts II and III of this book is a self-contained unit of information, so if a certain topic doesn't apply to you or you already have a handle on that part, there is no need for you to spend time on that chapter.

When you organize one area of your life, other problem areas often improve on their own. For example, when you unclutter and organize your space, you might find that your time management improves because you don't waste time looking for things. And when your time management improves, you're better able to focus on your priorities because you aren't so rushed. And when you focus on your priorities, you become more productive and effective! And when you're more productive and effective at work, you can be less stressed and more happy at home. So you can see how improving just one area of your life can directly affect other areas in a positive chain reaction.

Also, when you begin to organize one area of your office, your results motivate you to continue the process.

You can certainly read this book from cover to cover, but what I really want you to do is use it as a how-to manual for organizing the various aspects of your office. You might find that after you read Part I, have determined your primary work style, laid out the overview for your office, and begun thinking about the end result, you are so excited that you just want to dive in and get started before reading any further. Go for it!

Special Elements and Icons

I've done my best to arrange the material in this book so you can zero in on what you need. So, I've added some special elements to help you spot information:

- Some sections begin with a *You'll Need* list. This list will let you know whether you should have any supplies on hand as you read the section. If you have what you need as you read the chapter, you can complete the recommended steps right away, and you won't have to come back to do them later. To-do lists at the opening of many sections step you through the major steps of the sections' tasks.

- I've highlighted some information as *tips*. Tips indicate ideas, tricks, simple things you can do, or new ways for you to think that will help you as you move through the process of organizing your office.

- There are also *cautions* that give you a heads-up on what to watch out for in certain situations.

- *Notes* give you little tidbits of interesting information about the topic being discussed in the main body of text.

- At the end of each chapter, you'll find a *chapter summary* that summarizes and puts the major ideas of the chapter into a nutshell for you.

I've also included four special icons to help draw your attention to specific types of information:

- The *Client Success Story* icon indicates a real-life story about a client with a particular organizing challenge and how it was solved. Just as in that old television show, all names have been changed to protect the innocent.

- The *Fundamental Concept* icon precedes any reference to a key piece of information that can be applied in many areas of your life. For example, grouping like items with like items is a fundamental concept that applies whether you're organizing your kitchen, toy room, or office.

- The *It's Your Style* icon indicates a special note that offers a suggestion or idea for one of the four specific work styles identified in Part I.

- Staying organized for the long haul is all about maintenance. The *Maintenance Tip* icon appears next to examples of how to maintain systems, create habits, or make things run smoothly for the long term.

Our Goal

I know that if you are reading this book, you are probably overwhelmed by your current situation. This book is designed to help you get over the stumbling blocks that have been in your way until now.

- If you've tried various systems without success, this book will show you how to take control of your office space and organize it so you can be productive and feel successful.
- If you think you're too busy just getting through the day to find time to organize your office, that's a clue that you really need to! If you had extra time, you'd probably already be more organized.

My goal is to change your situation from harried, stressed, and drowning in paperwork to focused, organized, and more productive than ever!

Part 1

Getting Started

Determining Your Work Style

We're all human and, by our very nature, we are dynamic, interesting, and complex beings. We each have our own style of doing things. For example, you might get dressed in the morning from the top down, beginning with your shirt and working down to your shoes. Or perhaps you get dressed starting with your socks, then your slacks, and then your shirt. Or maybe you put your pants on first and the rest follows. In any case, the result is the same—you end up fully dressed—but it's your own dressing *style* that determines what order you put on your clothing. You have your own style for many elements in your life—the way you eat, drive, speak, walk, and write, just to name a few. You also have a style in the way you work. When you begin to notice your habits and tendencies, you can determine your primary work style.

In this chapter, you take and score a short quiz designed to help identify your own working style. After you know your primary work style, you can more effectively choose the organizational tools and systems that will work best for you. To determine your primary work style, take a few minutes to take the work style quiz in this chapter and to learn a bit about what its results can tell you.

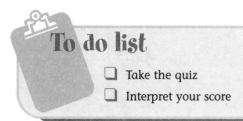

To do list

- ☐ Take the quiz
- ☐ Interpret your score

The Work Style Quiz

Circle the letter beside the most correct answer for each of the questions in this quiz. Answer each question honestly and without thinking about it for too long—your first impression is generally the truest representation and indicator of your style. Don't worry if you want to skip a question or two—you can come back to them when you're finished. There are no right or wrong answers, so the important thing is to be honest with yourself. One more thing to remember is that sometimes you will have more than one answer to each question. That's fine; just indicate which one is *most* true for you. If you really can't choose just one and have to circle two answers, that's okay, too, because most people aren't completely consistent in their habits. This quiz is not a scientifically created, written-in-stone assessment tool. It is a general indicator of what your primary working style is, and it will give you an idea of what strengths and challenges you'll take into the task of organizing your office.

Things You'll Need

- ☐ Pencil or other writing instrument

1. When preparing for a large project, I usually
   A. Do the research I need quickly, without taking extensive notes, preferring to remember everything in my head.
   B. Spend a lot of time sitting down to plan my schedule and plan deadlines for each section of the project. I gather all my materials in advance and make detailed, meticulous research notes.
   C. Put the project on the back burner until the week before it is due, or until someone reminds me about it.
   D. Gather the materials I need, and lay them on my desk or scatter them about the floor in piles.
   E. Create really attractive presentation materials, re-do my notes until they look perfect, and make binders with color-coded tabs for all the parts of my project.

2. In my work, I really enjoy

    A. Relationships with my customers/clients

    B. Research and/or data handling

    C. I don't enjoy my work at all

    D. Reading and processing information

    E. Regrouping, catching up, and maintaining order.

3. I tend to make decisions

    A. Quickly—and most often I am happy with my decisions.

    B. Very slowly and painstakingly, carefully considering each option and asking others for their input.

    C. I tend not to like to make decisions. I put them off until someone else makes them for me or the circumstance takes care of itself.

    D. I often feel overwhelmed by decision-making. Even after I've made a decision, I sometimes wonder if it was the right one.

    E. My decision-making style depends on the situation. Sometimes it's quick and other times I like to do more research and take my time.

4. I prefer

    A. A noisy, fast-paced work environment

    B. A quieter, academic, or scientific work environment

    C. An unstructured work environment where I can set my own schedule and work unsupervised

    D. A work environment where I feel free to spread out and have my personal art, awards, and family photos on display

    E. A sparsely appointed, orderly work environment

5. My professional background is in

    A. Sales or working with the public.

    B. Academia, science, finance.

    C. I have a varied background.

    D. Psychology, counseling, healthcare.

    E. Other.

6. If I *had* to choose my favorite out of the activities below, I'd choose

    A. Watching a hockey game

    B. Playing chess

    C. Watching a baseball game

     D. Attending a play

     E. Going to an art gallery

7. My desk normally looks like this:

     A. A mess of current, but unrelated, paper strewn about, including projects that I am in the middle of working on

     B. Piled high with papers, books, magazines, and other materials that are often very old or never referred to

     C. Full of unpaid bills and half-finished projects

     D. Covered with to-do lists, sticky notes, photos, and doodles

     E. Clean surfaces, but drawers that are full and often disorderly

8. I procrastinate

     A. Rarely, if ever.

     B. I don't intend to procrastinate, but sometimes it seems to just happen. Deadlines sneak up on me.

     C. I almost always put things off, regardless of the task size or complexity.

     D. I procrastinate on things that don't seem important at the moment, but then I regret it later.

     E. I put off about 25% of the decisions or actions I need to handle, depending on how difficult they seem.

9. I most enjoy

     A. Engaging in lively conversation or relaxing with friends

     B. Reading to learn

     C. Watching television

     D. Painting, drawing, or creating

     E. Reading for pleasure or doing household work

10. Clutter is

     A. Pretty stressful for me

     B. Strangely comforting to me

     C. Something I've accepted

     D. Simultaneously stressful and comforting

     E. Extremely stress-inducing

11. I believe

    A. Doing something halfway is better than not doing it at all.

    B. It is important to always make the absolute right decision.

    C. I work best under pressure.

    D. I can't find anything unless it's out and I can see it.

    E. An orderly environment is important to clear thinking.

12. I often find myself to be

    A. Impatient in traffic or while waiting in lines

    B. Thinking about the way things work, contemplating solutions to the world's problems

    C. Day dreaming or lost in my own thoughts

    D. Distracted by people, sights, or activities around me

    E. Distracted by noise and physical clutter

Scoring the Quiz

Add up the number of A's, Bs, and so on, keeping a list of the totals for each letter you chose. If you have a higher number of one letter than all the others, that gives you an idea of what your primary work style is. Bearing in mind that this assessment is based on observation of real-life clientele, the description of each work style might not describe you exactly. It will describe you and your habits to a large degree, however, and after you know your primary style, you can tailor your organizational solutions to fit your needs.

If you answered

- Mostly A's—Your primary work style is the Speed Demon.
- Mostly Bs—Your primary work style is the Ponderer.
- Mostly Cs—Your primary work style is the Scarlett O'Hara.
- Mostly Ds—Your primary work style is the Visual.
- Mostly Es—Your primary work style is the Aesthetic.
- Mostly evenly distributed answers—You're a combination of all these styles.

The following sections tell you more about each of these work styles, and the special challenges and advantages you'll face when you fall into one of them.

The Speed Demon

You think quickly, you speak quickly, and you probably love email because of its instant nature. When you get an idea into your head, you want to act on it immediately and you might get irritated by those around you who move more slowly than you do. You tend to enjoy doing more than one thing at a time and you like being on the go. You thrive when things are busy and you have a fairly high energy level. You are likely to be outgoing, you enjoy people, and you're good at networking, building business relationships, and maintaining friendships. Speed Demons are often found in sales, customer service, and consulting.

If you are a Speed Demon, you have a lot of strengths that help make you good at your job and its day-to-day tasks. But your working style presents a few speed bumps, too. Here are some of the challenges you face:

- You don't always recognize the value in taking a little bit of additional time to do something thoroughly—you often rush through tasks or shortcut your systems in an effort to save time and move on to your next activity or appointment. This shortcutting results in your having to come back and re-do things later that you didn't do quite right the first time.

- You also don't appreciate the value of follow-through systems. You believe in the *personal relationship* aspect of following through, and you're good at keeping in contact with old friends and past clients. However, the administrative aspect of follow through falls by the wayside. This means that you aren't ever sure when you last touched base with your customers unless it was so recently that you remember the conversation. Although you probably called on the phone to check in like a good relationship-builder does, you never take that extra second or two to note the phone call activity and conversation points into a tracking system for later reference.

- As a Speed Demon, you might also *overestimate* the accuracy of your memory and often find yourself at a loss for information or small details you didn't write down because you "thought you'd remember." Speed Demons can have trouble focusing on, and being fully present and paying attention to, the present moment because they are always eager to move on to the next thing on their list.

The Ponderer

You are likely a person of high intelligence and you enjoy the thought process. You enjoy debating and examining situations from various angles, and you have a tendency to mull things over for extended periods of time. You are likely to be a slow decision-maker and you'd rather make no decision than make the wrong one. You like books, paper, and anything else that is information-related or assists you in research. Ponderers are often found in the fields of academia, finance, or science.

If you're a Ponderer, your thoughtful approach to your work and life help to make you strong, careful, and attentive. But sometimes the Ponderer's slow and steady approach can have its drawbacks. Here are your challenges:

- You love information! It gives you comfort and you tend to keep a lot of it, mostly in the form of books or paper, which results in a cluttered space. You tend to collect information, even if it's old or outdated, because of your love for the written word and the comfort you get in knowing that information is at your fingertips.

- Your tendency to make slow decisions keeps you mired in clutter because one of the key factors in a person's ability to stay clutter-free is quick and confident decision-making. When decisions are made quickly, the physical clutter can be moved out quickly. When decisions are made slowly, however, the clutter accumulates faster than it is moved out and it begins to snow you under.

- The irony in being a Ponderer is that the very habit you enjoy—keeping a large volume of information so you can refer to it later—is precisely what *prevents* you from being able to find the information you need later. Yes, it's a vicious cycle.

IN THE OFFICE

Your office is a place you spend a great deal of time. Statistically, you'll spend a third of your life working, and why shouldn't your office be a space where you enjoy being? There's no rule that says work has to be conducted in a drab, uninviting space. There is no one single system that works for everyone or one right way to set up and organize an office, and isn't that comforting? If you are ready to make your office into a place you like to be, rather than a place you dread, and if you desire a workspace where you can feel successful and effective, good for you! The mindset with which you approach this project will largely determine your speed and success in getting organized. Taking advantage of your strengths and working *with* your primary work style, rather than *against* it, will also help you achieve powerful results the first time around!

The Scarlett O'Hara

If you think back to the movie *Gone With The Wind*, Scarlett O'Hara said, "I'll think about that tomorrow." If you're a Scarlett O'Hara, you often plan to think about things or do things tomorrow. We all procrastinate to a certain degree, and most people have just a few specific types of decisions or activities they put off, so their procrastination doesn't negatively affect their life or their work. If you are a Scarlett O'Hara, however, you are a habitual procrastinator and you tend to routinely put things off, without even considering the effects of a delayed action or decision.

Putting things off is your default way of handling even simple tasks that take only a little time to complete. You are always seeking an activity that is more fun, exciting, or interesting than what you know you should be doing. You have a false belief that if you put something off, it will be easier to do later, and your desire for instant gratification is strong.

Whether you want to believe it or not, ignoring the task at hand doesn't always pay off—for your work, your health, or your peace of mind. Before you say "fiddle-dee-dee" and move on, take a look at some of the challenges facing you if you fit the Scarlett O'Hara work style:

- Your procrastination is likely causing you stress in your personal life as well as at work because you might often work late trying to finish tasks or projects you had put off.

- You might be in the habit of procrastinating to the point that it is affecting your productivity, your effectiveness, and your job satisfaction. Left unaddressed, your procrastination habit could jeopardize your success, and could impact you so much that you have trouble keeping your job.

- Procrastination is also an insidious robber of your self-esteem and sense of accomplishment. By procrastinating, you sabotage your own success by putting things off until you don't have enough time to do them properly, so the results are less satisfactory than they could be.

The Visual

You believe that you have to see things in order to remember to act upon them, or to remember where they live. Your office is likely piled high with papers, files, books, and projects because you are afraid that if you file anything away, you'll never find it again. Your walls might be covered with bulletin boards, white boards, and papers. You might also have a photographic memory and you rely on it to find things by recalling where you last saw something. You also remember where on a piece of paper a bit of information is written, or on what color of paper it is written. You remember just what pile you have placed something in, even if you don't know exactly where in the pile it might be hiding. Visuals are often musicians, artists, designers, engineers, or architects.

Your creativity, energy, and style are a great benefit to you as you organize your office into a dynamic, efficient working space. But, as with every working style, this one offers a few challenges as well:

- Because you like to have everything "out and about" where you can see it, you sometimes have a hard time locating a specific piece of information due to all the clutter present. Your challenge is keeping things visible, yet orderly and easy to locate.

- You also believe that if you can't see it, you can't find it. This fear of losing things you can't see is unfounded. There are areas of your life where you don't see everything but can still function, such as your kitchen. You probably don't have all your pots, pans, glassware, and silverware sitting out on the countertops. They are hidden behind cabinet doors, yet you always know right where to find them, don't you? The same results can be created in your office, just by using the right organizing tools for your style and creating new habits to go along with the tools.

The Aesthetic

You value calm, peace, and order and you prefer open, clean spaces. This desire for open space means that you feel stressed when things are in physical chaos in your home or office. Your eyes continually seek an uncluttered spot to "land" and when they can't find one, you want to run from the room. To outsiders and co-workers, your office might seem the picture of order—until they peek inside the drawers, closets, and other closed spaces in your office.

Aesthetics appear to be totally organized to those around them, but if you share this work style, you probably know about some of these challenges it brings with it:

- Your eyes just can't take the chaos! You value clear spaces so much that you often, in a desperate attempt for order, shove things haphazardly inside of closets, cabinets, and drawers, just to get it out of your sight. Like a teenager "cleaning" his room by stuffing everything under the bed, you attempt to clean your office by hiding your clutter behind closed doors. However, your hiding habit comes back to bite you later when you can't find what you need in a timely manner.

> **caution** As your life changes, your priorities change, and you can change your habits as well. Simply because you've always done something the same way is no reason to stick with it if it's no longer working for you. Don't let fear of change keep you stuck in your old and ineffective habits.

- You might also be guilty of buying organizing and office tools based on what they look like, rather than how they function, which leads to frustration on your part and a lot of under- or unutilized tools gathering dust in the storage closet.

The Combination

If you find that your answers run the gamut between A and E, you might not have a distinct primary work style, but, like many people, you share characteristics common to a combination of two or more styles. For example, you might be a Speed Demon who is very Visual, with leanings toward the Ponderer's care and contemplation now and again. Or you might be a Scarlett O'Hara with strong Visual tendencies, and you like to have things piled up so you can see them in front of you, even though it's chaotic.

If you use a combination of styles, you'll want to really think through the ideas and systems you choose to help you get organized. Although using various colors might be a perfect filing system for someone who is highly Visual, think twice before using color in your filing system if you are also a Speed Demon. You might think that color is a wonderful tool for a Visual person like you, and you're right—usually it is. However, as a partial Speed Demon, you might become impatient when you discover you're out of the proper color folder and you grab whatever color is handy, just to get the information filed. The result? Your wonderful color-coded filing system breaks down.

tip
Remember, you're a dynamic human being, so be flexible with yourself when undertaking this organizing project. It always feels strange the first few times you try something new, so just hang with it and give it a chance.

Summary

In this chapter, you took the work style quiz to learn your primary work style. Whether you are a Speed Demon, Ponderer, Scarlett O'Hara, Visual, Aesthetic, or, like most of us, a combination of two or more styles, you have certain tendencies and strengths. The quiz might have validated things you already knew, or the results might have come as a surprise to you. Either way, the insight will aid you in undertaking this organizing project.

Knowing your work style helps determine how you proceed in organizing your office. If you're primarily a Speed Demon, you'll set things up a little differently than someone who is a Ponderer, and that's quite all right. Now that you have an idea of what your primary work style is, you're better equipped to handle your particular challenges and capitalize on your strengths when setting up your systems. Chapter 2 will help you create the "big picture" idea of how you want your office to look and function.

Creating Your Office Vision

2

Before you begin any multifaceted project, whether building a doghouse, planning a party, or driving cross-country, knowing your desired outcome is the best way to start. Imagine if you tried to drive from one side of the country to the other without having a good idea of where you'd like to end up. It seems ridiculous, doesn't it? Would you just point your car in the general direction of the opposite coast and start driving? You could certainly do that, but chances are you'd find yourself getting off course, taking side roads, and hitting roadblocks or detours that would slow you down. In fact, you might get so side-tracked that you'd stop and settle down before you even reached the other coast, simply because you began without a plan. It's been said that you can't get where you want to go until you *know* where you want to go.

When undertaking a project like organizing your office, it's important to choose which areas are your highest priorities to get organized and put a general plan in place, even if you don't intend to complete every aspect of the plan in one fell swoop. At least you will have given it some thought and created a picture in your mind of what you're shooting for. In this chapter, you learn the process for envisioning just what your organized office should look like, and how it should function. You learn how to assess the way

In this chapter:

* Determine the flow of work and information in your office, and define what "organized" means to you

* Figure out your ideal information flow and determine where and how you want to store information

* Set up activity and storage zones in your office

* Establish priorities for what to keep

work and information flows in and out of your office, and what types of activities and information make up that flow. You learn how to set up an effective plan for each area within your office to provide the best arrangement for your office activity and storage needs.

Things You'll Need

❑ Pencil and paper

Questions to Ask Yourself Before You Begin

Organizing your office is not an end in itself, but rather a means to several ends. It's a vehicle that can move you from where you are now—feeling stuck and over-whelmed—to where you would like to be, *wherever* that might be. It's important to understand that there is no real value in simply having an organized office. The real value lays in the *results* of your organized office—the increased probability of reaching your goals, the ability to be more effective, and increase your success and well-being at work. Neat rows of pens and tidy stacks of papers and books don't mean anything unless your habits, routines, and systems keep you organized and effective. As a first step in creating your organizational vision, ask yourself these questions:

1. What are the three most important purposes of my work? (Be specific.)
2. Am I as effective as I could be or would like to be in all of these purposes?
3. What specific things or situations are hindering my effectiveness in any or all of these areas?
4. In a perfect world, what would my workspace look and feel like?
5. How do I feel when I walk into my office now, and how would I prefer to feel when walking into my office?
6. What image is my office currently projecting to my colleagues and/or clients, and what image would I prefer to project?
7. What important goals could I strive for and achieve if I were more organized and therefore more effective?

As you answer the above questions, you might find yourself realizing things you hadn't before, such as how your workspace makes you feel inside. You might discover that although you thought you were doing okay in terms of productivity, you could be doing a lot better when you really consider it. These

> **note** It is helpful to write down your answers to these questions as you answer them so you'll have a guide to remind you if you lose your focus along the way.

realizations can be unnerving at first, but they are actually good opportunities to make positive changes.

I worked with a client named Mandy* who runs a business from her three-bedroom home she shares with her husband and two dogs. Upon my arrival at her home, I discovered she had set up her office in the smallest bedroom, which also had the smallest closet and the smallest window, offering very little view to the outside. I also discovered that next to the office there was a guest room, which was a larger space with a double window, a pretty view, and a much larger closet.

After some discussion, Mandy agreed with me that it made the most sense to swap the two rooms, making the smaller room into a guest room and using the larger, brighter, more functional room as the office. We sold the guest bedroom furniture, painted the larger room a beautiful color Mandy loved, and, using a little creativity and organizing skills, created an executive office space she is proud to spend time in.

Because Mandy rarely has houseguests who need the guest room, we chose to put a futon into the smaller room, rather than a bed. Using a futon instead of a bed makes the room into a multipurpose space where Mandy and her husband can listen to music, relax, and read. On the rare occasion that guests need a place to sleep, the futon folds easily out into a full-size bed.

This office space swap was important for two reasons. First, because the smaller room wasn't working as her office, and second, because it helped get Mandy into a success mindset. With her new and greatly improved office space, she looked successful, she felt successful, and she began to treat her home business as a serious enterprise, which increased her financial success and fulfillment.

*Not the client's real name.

Now that you understand your organizing efforts must be in pursuit of a higher goal, it's time to figure out what you have in the way of paper, information, and other items, and how it can all work for you.

To do list

- ❑ Assess the types and amounts of information that come into (and go out of) your office
- ❑ Sort the information and documents you currently have into categories for reference and action
- ❑ Draft a system for prioritizing tasks and managing workflow

Determining Your Work and Information Flow

Before you can figure out how paper and information should move through your office, you need to identify what routinely comes across your desk. Of course, there are thousands of different jobs in the world, so the information you deal with is unique, which is why there is no standard way to organize it. If you owned a produce market, you'd store and handle blueberries in a different way than you'd store and handle watermelons or bananas because their sizes, hardiness, and shelf lives are different. You'd also evaluate what was fresh and what was past its freshness and act accordingly, throwing away anything old or unusable.

In a way, information is the same as fresh produce. Some of it is critically action-oriented, some is not urgent but still requires action, some is for reference, and some is just plain junk you don't need to keep at all. Until you identify what comes across your desk and establish a policy for how to handle each type of information, it will all seem equally important to you. Creating a hierarchy helps you keep paper and other information from piling up needlessly, burying you, and creating more stress.

Things You'll Need

- ❑ Your mail
- ❑ Your magazines
- ❑ A note pad
- ❑ A pen
- ❑ Sticky notes

Identifying the Information You Receive and Sorting the Information You Have

Begin by listing the different items and types of information you receive on a regular basis. Include your mail, interoffice communications, publications, books, products, and anything else that might come across your desk in the span of a week. Try to remember every aspect of your business and its related paper or information. As you receive a new piece of paper or other information, add it to your list. After a few days you'll have a good handle on what paper and information you deal with regularly and where it is coming from.

At the same time you are analyzing the incoming items and paper, you'll want to address the already existing piles in your office because they are no doubt a big part of your disorganization. What kind of paper makes up the piles in your office? Is it one kind of information or several kinds mixed together? If you tend to let a single type of information pile up (such as invoicing) because you don't enjoy dealing with it, there is a relatively easy fix for that problem. Simply delegate the task of handling that information to someone else. Consider delegating to a staff member, but if that's not a realistic solution, remember that virtual assistants, bookkeepers, and other outside support staff are available for hire on a contract basis. If delegation isn't realistic or possible in your scenario, keep the information corralled in a single spot until you choose to handle it all in one fell swoop, perhaps monthly or quarterly, and be sure it doesn't get mixed with other kinds of information.

If your piles are a completely mixed bag of many different kinds of information, they will require serious sorting and categorizing, followed by organizing and storing. Begin the identifying and sorting process with each pile, dividing each one into smaller piles according to the category the information belongs to. For example, you might have categories called Financial, Insurance, Building Operations, Sales, Marketing Materials, and Client Information. Whatever your categories are, also add five additional piles called Action, Add to Database, Delegate, Trash, and Shred.

> **tip** The tasks you like to do least are also the ones you tend to forget about. Coincidence? I think not. To prevent these tasks from slipping through the cracks, try scheduling them into your calendar or day planner on a recurring basis to remind yourself to handle them. If you use an electronic planner, you can set an appointment that automatically reschedules month after month. If you use a paper planner, sit down and hand write the task in for the next twelve months to help you remember it.

> **tip** As you can tell by their names, these five additional piles— Action, Add to Database, Delegate, Trash, and Shred—are action-oriented, and therefore should not be mingled with the other categories, which are strictly reference piles.

As you break each mixed stack into its reference categories, set aside anything that requires action and put it on one of your five action piles. What you'll end up with when you're finished sorting is several reference piles, each named for a specific category, and five action piles.

Your reference piles will have any number of names, depending on what kind of business you're in. Don't worry so much about calling each pile the perfect name at the beginning; there will be time for that later. Just break the papers up into categories as you think of them.

On the general Action pile, put items that require you to act upon them either now or in the future. Don't worry about their timeline right now; simply group them together for the moment. These actions can be anything you want—for example, call, read, mail, sign, review, or research. To make things easier, think about what the *next action* is when you first discover each piece of paper. Take a second and write that next action someplace on the paper. This extra second of effort will make it easy to remember what the next action is when you revisit that paper later.

When organizing your life, remember that anything you can take a few extra seconds to do now, to help you remember or to eliminate a step later, is always worth doing! It's always better to invest an extra tiny bit of work in the present because it will pay off down the road in time, money, headaches, or effort saved.

On the Add to Database pile, put items that just require you to add them to your database, Rolodex, or address book. Keeping your database up to date, whether it is electronic or paper, is one of the most important things you can do for yourself and your productivity. It not only consolidates everyone's contact information in one spot, but it also keeps you from having to search desperately through old phone messages and scraps of paper for a telephone number or mailing address. After the information is added to your database, throw away the paper it was originally written on to reduce your paper clutter.

A single, easily functional database filled with accurate information is a real treasure to any business person. It makes your work life simpler because you always know all your contacts will be together and easy to find.

Place items on the Delegate pile if they require action, but it doesn't have to be your action. As you put items on this pile, take a second to think about what the next action will be and who should handle it. Quickly write the action and the person who will do the action right on the paper itself, such as "Donna—check pricing." This way when you come back later to sort this pile down even further, you will already know the specifics of what should happen to each piece. Without even thinking, you'll be able to tell that the next action needed on that piece of paper should be Donna checking the pricing.

Again, the small, two-second act of making the note to yourself in advance as you discover the paper will save you time and effort later.

caution Break the jotting habit.

Jotting is writing a phone message, or any information, for that matter, on the first random scrap of paper you can find. Admittedly, the back of an envelope *does* look inviting when you're in a pinch, but down the line when you really need to find that person's name, phone number, or directions to his office, chances are that envelope will be long gone and you'll be in a pinch again! Get a small spiral notebook to keep your phone messages, driving directions, and notes to yourself, and always keep it handy. When you need to find a note you scribbled in a hurry, at least you'll know where to begin to look for it.

caution It is vitally important not to shred documents prior to their destroy dates. To learn more about destruction dates, check your company's document retention policy. If your company doesn't have a document retention policy, check with your professional service people, such as your accountants, attorneys, financial planners, and other people who are familiar with the laws and regulations of your industry. We will address creating a document retention policy in Chapter 3, "Creating the Office Framework."

Items should go on the Trash pile if they are no longer valuable, relevant, important, or necessary. Anything that has personal information included on it should go into the Shred pile. Understanding what to shred is important because identity theft is a growing—and profitable—business. Recent statistics claim that as many as seven million Americans each year become victims of identity theft, and the Federal Trade Commission speculates that the numbers will continue to rise.

PREVENTING IDENTITY THEFT

According to the Federal Trade Commission, if a thief fraudulently opens a credit card or takes out a loan in your name, the average amount in damages will be between $10,000 and $11,000—and that's just the average.

Along with those frightening statistics, if you are a victim of identity fraud, you should also anticipate spending between 20 and 60 hours of your precious time and $500–$1,200 of your money to clear your good name.

One way to make it tougher on identity thieves, be they outside contractors, current employees, or people unaffiliated with your company, is to be diligent about shredding. You should set up a document destruction schedule to have appropriate documents shredded on a regular basis. Anything that contains personal or sensitive information about yourself, your employees, or your customers and clients should be destroyed. Below is a sample list of some of the information you'll want to be sure to shred when its destroy date arrives. This is not a complete list by any means, but it will give you a good idea of the many types of information that should be shredded after their destroy dates have passed:

- Bank statements
- Financial statements
- Canceled checks
- Healthcare records
- Insurance records
- Credit reports
- Payroll records
- Confidential client information
- Business receipts
- Contracts

Applying Logic To Workflow

After you've assessed and sorted the information you deal with on a regular basis, it's time to figure out how to keep the piles from growing large and looming again. The difference between cleaning up an office and organizing it is that when you clean up, you are simply making things look tidy. Sure, you might throw some things away and make decisions you've been putting off, and that's always a positive thing! However, if you're just making the space look tidy and not setting up systems or routines that are simple to use and easy to maintain, you'll just get stuck cleaning up again and again.

Setting up systems means creating homes for things and information to live and a workflow in your office that will keep you organized for the long term. You also want to take the time to think through the systems you set up so they'll be easy to maintain. Just as cars are manufactured on an assembly line, with each piece of the car progressing in logical order through the process until it reaches its final destination, paper and information should have a process to flow through as well.

> **note** I recommend that businesses use an outside company to do their shredding. Choose a company that will come to your site and shred right there on location, as opposed to a company that will take your information away to shred it. Make sure you choose a company that guarantees to provide you with a certificate of destruction for each shredding session. Outsourcing this task not only eliminates the need for buying and maintaining shredding equipment, but it also reduces your company's liability because it limits unauthorized users' accessibility to confidential and classified information.

Imagine your office is a water system, where information flows through various pipelines like water through pipes. When a pipe becomes blocked, water backs up and causes all kinds of plumbing problems. Similarly, you can imagine that paper that doesn't have an assigned path can quickly become a clog in the pipes, creating a backlog. Clogs in your workflow system create disorder and stress, as well as negatively affect your productivity and success.

Effective workflow is largely determined by using four criteria based on what, which, how, and where:

- What action is required
- For which information
- How frequently it should happen
- Where that information should live during and after the process

Now that you have sorted your paper into your reference categories and action-oriented piles, begin further breaking down the pile called Action. You'll be sorting the Action pile into smaller categories just like you broke the other piles down. Each smaller pile will be labeled with a specific action, such as Review or Read. To come up with names for your specific action piles, just ask yourself, "What is the *next action* that needs to happen?" Use the first verb or action phrase that comes into your head to name your pile. Your first pile might be called something as simple as Follow Up or something as quirky as Reach Out and Touch. No matter; you should use the language that feels best to you, even if it seems silly or unorthodox.

BE SPECIFIC ABOUT ACTIONS

When choosing your list of actions to implement in your office, be careful not to be vague, using weak action words such as Do, Complete, or Work On. You might be tempted to use these words, while promising yourself, "I'll remember what that means." You have the best intentions, but I guarantee you won't remember later! When choosing your action words, be conventional, be unconventional, or be creative, but above all, be *specific*. Use specific action words such as Call, Read, Sign, Mail, or use complex phrases such as Read, Sign, and Send to Corporate Office. These are examples of specific actions that leave no question as to their meaning. I have such specific actions written in my office that it's almost funny. One of them is Receipts to Be Journal-Entried and Then Filed. Another says Medical Receipts to Be Reimbursed. Laugh if you must, but I love having that specific language to remind me. Plus, you can believe that nothing ever goes into those action spots by mistake!

To help you create your workflow system, make a simple table like the following one and list in the center column each type of information you discover. Note whether it is paper or electronic, and then in the right column, write what regular action is required for each one. Some items will require more than one action, in which case, just list all the actions required until the information gets put to rest. You can make a table like this in just a few minutes and hang it in a spot where you can refer to it easily. This way, when you have a question about how to deal with items or information, you have a handy guide to remind you of your plan. Another advantage to making your office organized and simple to work in is that if you are ill or out of town, someone else could come into your space and easily find important information or keep the business running in your absence without too much trouble.

Paper or Electronic	Type of Information	Action(s) Required
Paper	Sales reports	Review and file for reference if necessary
Paper	Meeting minutes	Review and file for reference if necessary
Paper	Lead sheets	Contact leads/set appointments
Paper	Insurance policies	Review and file for reference
Paper	Bills	Pay and file for reference
Paper	Magazines	Read and destroy
Paper	Receipts	Collect and submit with expenses
Paper	Expense reports	1. Complete by fifth of month and mail 2. File paid report with check stub
Paper	Solicitations	Trash without opening
Either	Ad copy and artwork	1. Review and return with changes 2. Review and approve or submit more changes 3. Review and approve
Electronic	Sales meeting notices	Review and schedule into calendar
Electronic	Monthly Web update	Prepare and upload to website
Electronic	Recruiting letter	Prepare and send to email list
Electronic	Email	1. Assess the priority or need for action 2. Respond or act immediately if possible 3. Move to a named electronic folder for later reference or delete original
Electronic	Client inquiries	1. Respond and file electronically 2. Follow up with sales call

In creating this table, you might discover that you don't really have a clear-cut idea of what to do with some of the paper that comes into your office. This discovery sheds some light on the cause of those pesky piles, doesn't it? You see, when you don't know what to do with something, chances are you'll put it into a pile to deal with later, at which time you *still* won't know what to do with it, so it stays in that pile until the end of time. This is where your table comes into play. If you have items listed on the

tip When setting up systems for items that need to be delegated, it's a good idea to designate a spot for each person's information to live until it is transferred to them. You could use a set of stacking trays, each one with a name label. When you need to hold something for someone else, just pop it into the appropriate tray and deliver it all at once.

table that have no action assigned to them in the right column, your job is to figure out the action. Remember, there is always someone you can ask who can help you learn the current acceptable flow of information or can help you set up a flow if one doesn't exist. It might be a more experienced co-worker, your boss, or an industry expert who can make recommendations on the ultimate fate of information after it passes through your hands.

After you have the actions written in the right column of your table, you can begin setting up the systems to support those actions. For example, let's say you own an auto mechanic shop and your table included an item such as Client Car Keys. Client car keys are certainly important items and they should have an action trail they follow from the time they leave the client's hand to the time the client picks up her car after the service has been completed. Failing to put a system in place for car keys to follow could mean disastrous results, such as losing the keys and having to have them remade, which would cost your company time and money and undoubtedly lead to a very unhappy customer.

To set up the system, you'd first figure out who is the first person to receive the keys. Let's say the first person to handle the keys is the front desk clerk. Then you identify who the next person in the chain is. In this case, it isn't a person at all, but rather a team of people, namely the auto mechanics who work in your shop. When putting a flow system in place, first look at who the people are in the work chain and then figure out how to best move the information from one person to the next without errors. So now that you know the keys have to move from the clerk to the mechanics team, you just have to figure out how to make it work in a simple fashion.

The simplest solution would be for the clerk to place keys a customer drops off into one designated spot where the mechanics could pick them up. The designated spot should be convenient for the mechanics to see and access, large enough to accommodate several sets of keys at once, and safely located so the keys don't accidentally get lost. The ideal system could be as simple as a clear plastic shoebox screwed into the wall and labeled Keys Coming In. The mechanics would be trained to check the box when they are finished working on a car, and if there are keys in the box, it means a car has arrived and is waiting to be fixed. To make the system even more precise, you could set up a row of hooks on the wall and hang each new customer's keys on a hook, beginning at the left side. You'd implement a system where keys hanging to the left are the first ones received and, therefore, they get attended to first. This way, the mechanics team knows which automobile has come in first and to work in the appropriate order. This example has just shown you how simple it is to figure out a workflow for each item or type of information you have to handle, if you just sit down and give it some thought in advance.

So, to recap, when planning workflow

1. Determine the action(s) required

2. Determine the people involved in the action, if applicable

3. Use the simplest and best system to facilitate the desired action

4. Communicate the proper and expected use of the system to those who will be implementing it

It is always easier to anticipate problems that could arise and design systems to address those problems in advance, rather than waiting until a negative situation forces you to become more organized. Anticipate what challenges might arise when you get busy and design your system with them in mind.

To do list

- ❏ Determine the best place for storing each type of information in your office
- ❏ Choose documents to be filed for later reference
- ❏ Create (or familiarize yourself with) a document-retention policy that fits your business and industry, state, and federal regulations

Deciding Where Your Information Should Live

You can figure out the most logical home for each type of information just by thinking through the action or flow it will go through. For example, let's say your job entails keeping receipts for expenses, and you see that your table listing says the procedure is to save those receipts and submit them with your expense report. Your next thought should be, "What simple system can I create so I have a handy place to keep receipts until I need them again?"

Then look at your office space, and choose a convenient spot for the receipts to live together until they are needed again—sort of like a waiting room for receipts. This "waiting room" might be something as simple as an envelope fastened with a magnet to the side of your filing cabinet, or a spindle sitting on your credenza. Wherever you choose to store receipts, be sure it is easy to access and that you use that spot consistently, so when the time comes to sit down and fill out expense reports, you know exactly where to look for those receipts. After you determine the most logical flow of information through your office, you'll have a better idea of where each type should live to ensure the appropriate accessibility.

For those who are heavily Visual, consider keeping your "waiting rooms" in places you can see easily, such as on clipboards or in stacking trays.

The most basic definition of *organization* is knowing what you have and being able to find it quickly when you need it. Period. It's an equation that requires both elements in order to work. If you don't know what you have, you risk re-acquiring it, which wastes time, effort, and money. On the other hand, if you do know what you have, but you don't know where to find it, you might as well not have it at all. Both parts of the equation work in tandem to create the state of being organized.

Keeping Files for Later Reference

Information and paper whose life cycle terminates in your office will quickly pile up unless you know what to keep versus what you can safely throw away. If your office is the end of the line for an item, your options are to either throw it away or file it away for later reference.

Let's look at the ramifications of each option. Throwing the item away is certainly the easiest option. If you're not sure of the value of the information or what to do with it, though, you are not likely to feel comfortable throwing it away, nor should you, at least not until you know it is safe to do so.

Filing is appropriate for paper information only if you're sure that it has present or future value. Filing should *never* be the default decision for anything you're not sure about. It's far easier to simply file something away instead of making a real decision about it, but in the long run, it's more time and cost effective to make the right decision the first time. Statistics show that you will only refer to about 20%–25% of what you ever file, so filing space should be reserved for things that you are fairly certain you'll need at a later time.

caution Be judicious about what paper you file away. Anything filed that could or should be destroyed takes up precious space in file drawers, as well as costs you labor dollars to maintain. Also, bloated files cost your company money per square foot to store. Aim to keep your files lean and mean.

Acting on it is another option, but what if it is something new or you just don't know what to do with it? You can ask someone at your company who is more experienced than you are, you can ask your boss (unless you *are* the boss), or you can ask one of your service professionals, such as your accountant or attorney. If there is no precedent, you could create one using the guidance of your boss, accountant, attorney, or other industry experts.

Keeping Information Long Term

There are some types of information that should never be discarded or shredded. Of course, your industry standards will determine what these are to a large degree. However, there are also general categories of information that should be archived indefinitely. Following is a sample list (not a complete list), but it will give you a good start:

- Anything relating to a lawsuit
- Anything relating to an insurance claim
- Articles of incorporation

- Corporate meeting minutes
- Tax returns
- Documents proving payments of debts
- Deeds to properties
- Audit records
- Contracts
- Copyright and trademark records
- Patents
- Retirement and pension records

 note For more information regarding document retention, refer to these Internet resources:
- American Institute of Certified Public Accountants www.aicpa.org
- National Federation of Independent Business www.nfib.com/page/home.html
- Sarbanes-Oxley Compliance Journal http://www.s-ox.com
- Securities and Exchange Commission www.sec.gov

For a more complete list, check with an accountant in your state, or your industry's governing body or professional association.

If you find that your company's document retention policy is more lenient than state, federal, or industry regulations, opt to go with the more stringent of the two time frames. If your company's policy is the more stringent one, abide by it, but also encourage review of that policy each year to be sure documents aren't being kept longer than necessary.

To do list

☐ Divide your office into activity zones
☐ Determine what materials and equipment should be located in each zone

Setting Up Zones in Your Office

Have you ever been inside a preschool? If so, you might have noticed that there are specific areas where different activities happen. There is an arts and crafts area, an area where kids can play with toys, a nap area, and an area for meals.

In the art area, the children have tables and chairs set up where they can draw, paint, and color. Their art supplies, such as paints, crayons, and pencils, are stored near the art area. The meal zone has a place for each child to sit and eat, and has the items necessary for meal preparation and storage close by. Organizing the space in this manner allows the preschool to function smoothly by grouping children into different areas according to what activity they are doing and by storing the necessary materials for those activities in or near the designated areas.

You can set up your office in zones as well, with some zones designated as office activity zones, while others are for storage. Breaking your office into Zones One, Two, and Three according to frequency and ease of use will give you a heightened sense of clarity when you work. It will be in sharp contrast to how you are currently storing things in your office. It will also make you question *why* you keep so much paper and clutter. When you begin working in a zoned office, you'll experience the benefits of having the things you need most often at your fingertips while everything else is out of the way until you need it.

Identifying Zone One

Zone One is what I call "prime real estate." If you were selling homes in California, this would be your beachfront property. In your office, Zone One is comprised of the primary areas you can reach from a sitting position. Zone One areas include

- Your desktop
- Your hutch, if you have one
- The shallow drawers in your desk
- The file drawers in your desk

These areas are the ones that should hold your most important and most often accessed information and items. Take a look right now at your desktop. What do you see there? Are there items on your desktop that you haven't touched in months? Are books and reference materials that you rarely refer to taking up space there? Is your phone on your desk and if so, do you consider it a key piece of equipment that absolutely needs to live there? These are the kind of questions to ask yourself when allocating Zone One space in your office. You wouldn't put a pet resort on beachfront property, and the last thing you want to do is fill up your prime office real estate with things that don't merit living there.

Now that you've sorted and organized the piles of paper in your office, move on to the other items that are taking up space on your desktop. Pull everything except your computer off your desk and put it on the floor or on a conference table across the room so you have a nice clear space to start. Assess each item before putting it back onto the desk again, remembering that your prime real estate should only be used for storing items you use most often.

Here is a sample list of items that might live in your Zone One space:

- Computer, keyboard, and monitor
- Regularly used reference manuals or books
- Telephone
- Pens, pencils, highlighters, and markers
- Calculator

- PDA or planner
- Important and often accessed paper files
- Business cards
- Stapler
- Paper and information you need frequently
- Your action files

The prime real estate in your space should always be reserved for the information and items you use most often and need close at hand on a regular basis.

Identifying Zone Two

If Zone One is your beachfront property, Zone Two is the street one block back from the beach. It's still easy access to the beach, but not quite as valuable. Zone Two is the spaces in your office that are fairly easily accessible but not necessarily reachable from a sitting position. Zone Two will require you to swivel your chair backwards or stand up to access the items stored there, but it's okay by virtue of the fact that it's Zone Two space and you shouldn't need to access it every day, anyway.

Zone Two encompasses the following areas:

- The wall space next to or behind your desk
- Your credenza
- Your lateral file cabinet
- Any furniture across the room from your desk
- The supply closet in your office

When thinking about Zone Two and what should live there, consider how you use the items in your office. If you maintain paper personnel files but you don't often have the need to refer to them, it's a safe bet they could live in a Zone Two space, such as a lateral filing drawer on the other side of your office. On the other hand, if you are a recruiter and you constantly refer to your personnel files to pull résumés and whatnot, Zone Two is probably not the best place for them to live; consider moving them into Zone One space for easy, frequent access. It's simple to decide what should live in Zone One versus what should live in Zone Two. Just think about the frequency of use and the need for accessibility and that will tell you which zone is most appropriate.

Here is a sample list of things that might live in your Zone Two space:

- Computer software disks
- Blank media, such as blank CD-ROM disks
- Stocked office supplies
- Printer paper and ink
- Peripherals (printers, scanners, and fax machines)
- Business stationery and envelopes
- Reference books not often used
- Mailing and packaging materials
- Catalogs or product literature

Identifying Zone Three

If Zone Two is the one block back from the beach, Zone Three is ten blocks off the beach, where the properties still have beach access but it takes a lot more walking to get there. Your Zone Three is your offsite storage facility, your supply closet on a different floor, or your basement. Zone Three is not necessarily easily accessible and it doesn't even have to be in the same building or city as your office. Zone Three is where your archival files, old company documents, paperwork waiting for destruction, and anything else you might need access to should live, but the odds are remote you'll need it.

If you work for a company that has several regional or satellite offices, your Zone Three storage might be located in one of those buildings. It might be a storage closet in the basement or it might be the entire basement. Remember that Zone Three is not a dumping ground, so don't treat it as such. Zone Three is still space your company pays for by the square foot, and only things that really need long-term storage should be permitted to live there. Here is sample list of what might live in your Zone Three space:

- Archival paper files
- Old company financial records and tax returns
- Historic personnel files
- Company history, such as clippings or newsletters
- Overstocked furniture not presently in use
- Computer equipment not presently in use
- Bulk quantities of current promotional items/materials

Some years ago I worked with a company that produced, duplicated, and sold audio and videotapes. They also held special fund-raising weekend retreats, for which they produced high-quality promotional brochures. Their Zone Three storage was half of the entire second floor of their building. It was a huge, empty concrete walled space that held years of archived files, old furniture, outdated promotional materials, and everything else with which they didn't know what to do. I spent months up there organizing the things they needed to keep and getting rid of things they had been storing unnecessarily. In the end, I had a pile of trash I estimate would have filled the back of two dump trucks, most of which was extra brochures for the weekend retreats that had long since been over. The result of my hard work was a lot of free space in their storage area that they could use for future archiving of materials and information.

Remember that your Zone Three should not be a paperwork graveyard where you send things you're not sure about. It should be a legitimate, organized storage space where you can go to find something archival if you really need it.

Setting Priorities

Setting priorities is a bit like triage in an emergency room. When the hospital emergency room is filled with patients all awaiting treatment, triage is the method they use to determine the priority of each injury and who should be treated first, versus who can safely be treated later. To run triage in your office, you have to determine where on the priority scale your tasks and paperwork fall. If the information in question is time sensitive, such as a meeting notice, event invitation, or a project whose deadline is looming, its priority should be high and it should be acted upon quickly. In the case of a meeting, you would note the meeting in your calendar along with any important details, such as directions or materials needed, and then discard the actual notice itself. Some contact managers and electronic calendars allow you to move or copy an email directly into a specific time on your calendar, making it into an appointment. With an invitation to an event, you'd do the same, noting any additional information on your calendar and discarding the invitation itself, unless you'll need it to gain entrance to the event.

Papers related to a project with an upcoming deadline should be placed into your Action file and the action steps noted on your calendar. Scheduling specific time to complete tasks helps you stay focused and on task.

If a piece of paper or information needs to travel from your desk to someone else's desk, its priority should be high and therefore should be delegated quickly. You don't want to be

> **tip**
> Filing would be a great task to be delegated to an assistant or other staff member. Depending on the familiarity of that person with your files, you may want to write the name of the file in the upper corner of each item to be filed.

responsible for causing someone else to get a late start on a project by holding it too long at your desk. By handing off materials quickly, you set the other person up for success.

Another factor that plays into setting priorities is the purpose of the information at hand. Does the paper or information being acted on impact your primary purpose right now? If you have a clear picture of what your highest and best use of your time is at any given moment, you will rarely have trouble prioritizing. If your main purpose at your company is sales, it's pretty obvious that anything that will positively impact your ability to make a sale is the most important thing to be working on at the moment.

If your main purpose is customer support, doing administrative work would naturally fall to secondary priority status. In order to do administrative work, you'd be neglecting your main purpose of supporting the customer. If you aren't clear on what your priorities should be, or what the company's expectations are as to your job function, it's important to ask your boss to clarify those issues. This way you have a good understanding of the appropriate hierarchy of your various tasks and you know that you're on the same page as the higher-ups in your company. Setting priorities can get a little hairy when things are busy, and several things seem to be equally important and pulling for your time. If this is the case, it pays to stop and take a few seconds to think through and figure out what is the highest priority. But how do you accomplish that when *everything* feels important?

Ask yourself the following questions:

1. Will delaying or eliminating the task have a negative consequence? If so, how severe is the consequence?

2. Does the task have a firm deadline or a flexible one?

3. Is someone else waiting for you to act before he can begin his own work? If so, what are the possible consequences of his work being delayed?

4. Does this task further a goal or contribute to your primary purpose at work?

5. Can this task be delegated, and if so, to whom?

These questions will help you sift through and effectively prioritize items that seem to all be of the same importance. Taking the small amount of time required to prioritize will pay off for you because it allows you to focus on those tasks that further your most important goals, while saving other tasks for later or delegating them to others.

Summary

In this chapter you began to create the vision for your office by thinking about the many kinds of information that come across your desk for you and your staff to handle. You got rid of the backlog of paper piles in your office by sorting them into reference and action piles, and then further sorting your action piles so each pile had a specific action attached to it. Even better, you uncovered any lurking but important action items or projects that might have been buried and languishing in the mystery piles.

After you sorted your backlog of paper, you learned how to set up logical systems that would make your work easily and effectively flow through your space. You also learned some tips to help you prioritize paper and tasks so you can be more effective in the time you spend working. In Chapter 3 we'll address setting up the framework and layout of your office from both an aesthetic and functional point of view.

Creating Your Office Framework

3

When undertaking a large project, it makes sense to first address the largest aspects, get those pieces in place, and then move to the smaller, more detailed aspects of the project. A bit of planning on the front end sets you up for success in any project, whether you are painting a landscape or organizing your office. In an office setting, there are large framework factors to consider before you get down to the nitty-gritty detail work of organizing the drawers, nooks, and crannies in your office.

These large framework factors are the subject of this chapter. Here, you learn how to organize and decorate your office space (based on its size), choose the appropriate furniture for your space and needs, select the flooring style that works best for you, and decide upon the proper color scheme and lighting for your working style and profession. Because you spend so much time in your office, it's important that you feel comfortable and enjoy your time there. Toward that end, this chapter also helps you learn how to accommodate plants and other personal objects in your office.

In this chapter:

* Choose the appropriate furniture for your needs
* Create a scale model to find the best office layout with the least amount of effort
* Learn the importance of color and lighting, and choose a color scheme that matches your personal and professional style
* Select the best window and floor treatments for your personal and professional preferences
* Learn how to accommodate plants and office-appropriate pets
* Consider which—and how many—personal items you want to keep in your office

To do list

- ☐ Choose primary furnishings that match your working style and workflow
- ☐ Consider the type of desk, working surfaces, and desktop storage that fits your office size and needs
- ☐ Find an office chair that fits and supports your body

Choosing Your Primary Furniture

Primary furniture consists of your desk, work surfaces, and your chair. Secondary furniture is anything additional, such as filing cabinets, conference tables, guest chairs, or shelving units; these items are addressed in other chapters throughout the book. Your primary furniture is one of the most important elements in your office. Your desk serves as a place for working, as well as storage of Zone One items, and it is the keystone of your office (you learned about assigning and using Zones in your office in Chapter 2, "Creating Your Office Vision").

Your chair is the tool you use most in conjunction with your desk and it is equally important. If your office has been furnished by your current employer, you might have had no choice about the furniture in your office when you took your job. If it isn't working for you, however, it is in your best interest—and ultimately the company's best interest—to replace it with furniture that works for you. If you're self-employed, it's even more important because any time you're nonproductive you're losing income. When evaluating your present office furniture, examine your options by asking yourself the following questions:

- Do I have enough flat work surfaces?
- Do I have plenty of room to use my computer and keyboard comfortably?
- Is my chair a comfortable height and does it support me on even the longest days?
- Will my company allow me to change my furniture, even if I purchase it myself?
- What storage or functional aspects would I want new furniture to have that my present furniture is missing?

> **tip**
>
> When thinking about your office furniture, you'll need to remember to create dedicated space for working at your computer, doing administrative or other paper work, and completing various projects. Review "Setting Up Zones in Your Office" in Chapter 2, and then take these space needs into account when determining how much flat surface area to create.

- Are there pieces in my office that are being underutilized or have become stacking spots for paper?
- Do I have space to hold all my paper files?

Choosing a Desk and Desktop Storage

The way you work and the items and information in your office determines the style of desk you need. If your work is paper-intensive and your projects require a large amount of flat work space, consider using a desk with a return. A *return* is the second piece of furniture that makes a desk L-shaped, as shown in Figure 3.1. This additional piece is used to add extra work space.

FIGURE 3.1

An L-shaped desk and return combination offers additional work and storage space.

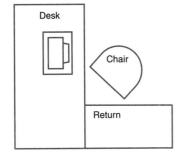

If your work requires you to refer to books, manuals, or other reference materials, consider purchasing a desk with a hutch on top for storing those items close at hand. A hutch is a great way to keep materials nearby without losing any of your work surface. Figure 3.2 shows a desk with a hutch that includes two rows of shelves.

FIGURE 3.2

The hutch above the desk offers extra storage for items used frequently and needed close at hand.

If you work from a cubicle, you might not have the ability to add a hutch to your desk. However, many desks situated in cubes automatically come with closed overhead cabinet space. This additional storage is great for keeping reference materials, books, and binders nearby without losing any work space on your desktop.

There are also desks that fit across the corner of a room, as shown in Figure 3.3. Corner desks give you the option to place a hutch on top in the center. A corner desk is a great way to utilize a small office, while still leaving space for additional furniture in the center or other side of the room.

FIGURE 3.3

A corner desk creates open space in the center of the office for traffic flow.

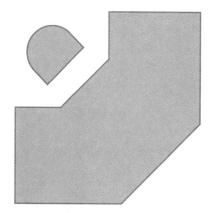

Selecting the Right Office Chair

The chair you choose is important, especially if you spend most of your time in your office, rather than out in the field. A quality desk chair that fits you well will make a big difference in the way your body feels at the end of each day, which contributes either positively or negatively to your effectiveness and productivity.

Never buy a chair without spending several minutes sitting in it first. Each chair will feel different to you, and before you spend a dime you want to be sure the chair is comfortable and meets your needs. Be sure the chair you choose has several options for adjustment. You should easily be able to change the height of the seat and back, as well as the armrests. Many chairs offer adjustable tension settings on the backrest that enable you to determine how much pressure it takes to recline. Check for adjustable lumbar settings as well, so you can set the chair to support your lower back comfortably.

tip Set the overall height of your chair so you can comfortably use your mouse and keyboard when working at the computer. If you can't put your feet on the floor when your chair is at the proper height, consider getting something to rest your feet on. Using a footrest reduces muscle fatigue by taking pressure off your lower back and will keep pressure off the back of your legs.

The bottom line is that if you use an office chair that doesn't offer you adequate comfort and support, you are needlessly subjecting yourself to pain and stress that could easily be avoided. It's worth spending extra money on a higher-quality chair that will eliminate the back pain and other physical stresses an inadequate chair could cause.

To do list

- ❑ Create a scale drawing of your office
- ❑ Learn to achieve maximum function with minimum furniture
- ❑ Plan for traffic flow and place furniture accordingly
- ❑ Place office equipment and peripherals

Using a Scale Model to Lay Out Your Office

It's important to know how much actual space you have to work with before you jump into creating (or re-creating) your office. Keep in mind that you're striving to create a comfortable work space with good traffic flow. Looking through catalogs and finding items you love is the easy part. If you don't know how much room you're working with, however, you could spend a lot of money on furniture that doesn't work for you. Buying first and measuring later means your furniture might end up being too large or too small for the room. This is why it's worth taking a little time to make a basic scale drawing of your room. The scale drawing gives you a great foundation from which to begin adding and moving office furniture. Using a scale-model floor plan and paper cutouts of furniture and equipment is the best way to try out different plans before you commit to one. Plus, you avoid hauling furniture around the room, trying various configurations until you get it right. Moving paper cutouts is a whole lot easier than moving furniture!

Things You'll Need

- ❑ Tape measure
- ❑ Graph paper
- ❑ Mechanical pencil
- ❑ Ruler or other straight-edge device
- ❑ Scissors
- ❑ Sticky notes

Measuring and Creating Scale Drawings

A scale model or scale drawing is a rendition of something large, reduced in size but proportionally accurate. To create a drawing of your office, measure the space using a tape measure. To get the most accurate measurements for your scale drawing, measure the entire *length* of each wall first, noting it on paper, and then measure *across* the room to double-check your numbers. After you have your measurements written down, use your graph paper and mathematically figure out how many squares you want to be equivalent to one foot. Choose this ratio based on the overall size of your graph paper and the drawing size you'll need in order to sketch in furniture and equipment placement.

Let's say your room is 20' × 14' and you are using graph paper with 1/4" squares. A scale of 1/2" (two squares) to a foot means that a 20-foot wall would convert to a 10-inch line on your paper. Using a scale of 1/2" to a foot gives you plenty of room to write and makes the drawing large enough to easily see each element. If your room is relatively small, go ahead and use a larger scale of 1" per foot. Even though you won't need to write anything more than the names of each item and its dimensions, the larger you make your scale, the more room you'll have to make these notes on the floor plan. After you've chosen your scale, be sure to note it somewhere on the paper so you can remember it later. For example, jot a note on the floor plan that says, "One inch = one foot."

Now that you've chosen your scale, draw the outline of your room using your graph paper and straight edge.

After you have drawn the lengths of the walls on your graph paper, measure and draw in the locations of the door openings and windows; also indicate on your drawing where the phone jacks and outlets are located. Remember to draw your window and door openings to scale so you can accurately see how everything fits together on paper. The scale drawing in Figure 3.4 shows a 14' × 16' office drawn on graph paper using two squares for each linear foot. The doors, windows, outlets, and jacks have been added to scale in this drawing.

Now that you have your physical space outlined to scale on graph paper, you're ready to move on to the next step, which is considering the furniture layout of your office.

> **tip**
> It is helpful to look through magazines to find photos of offices that inspire you. You certainly don't need to replicate any one office, but you can choose specific elements from each photo you like and combine them to make your space new and unique.

FIGURE 3.4
This drawing shows the added elements of windows, doors, closet space, outlets (which are shown as a circle with two lines intersecting), and phone jacks (which are shown as triangles).

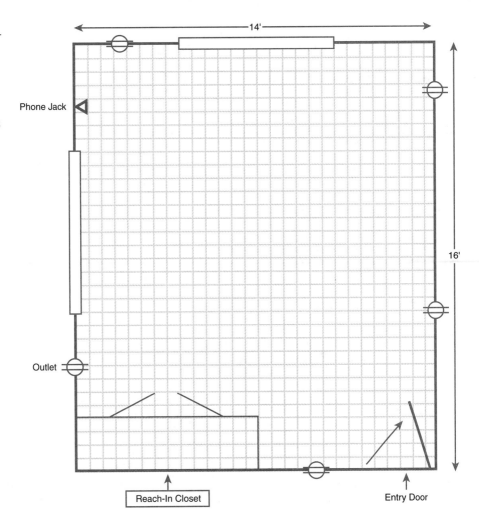

Phone Jack

Outlet

Reach-In Closet

Entry Door

14'

16'

Creating Furniture Cutouts

Now you're ready to begin testing office arrangements using paper cutouts to represent your primary office furnishings. Cutting out scale models of your furniture gives you an easy way to rearrange the elements of the room without doing any hard work. The beauty of it is you don't have to guess what it will look like or how much space you'll have left over because your model is created to tell you those things by virtue of the fact that it is built to scale.

Make your paper cutouts by measuring your present furniture, converting that measurement to the scale you've chosen for your drawing, and then cutting its shape to that size out of a sticky note. To convert actual size furniture to a cutout, just refer to your scale. Using a scale of 1/2" equals 1', a desk 5' by 2' would convert to a paper cutout of 2 1/2" by 1". Cut the model out of the sticky note, write the word *desk* on it and write the desk dimensions on the cutout as well. Be sure to use the sticky end of the note when cutting out your shape so it will stick to the graph.

When you place this two-dimensional scale model of your desk on your graph floor plan, you'll see how it looks exactly in proportion to the size of the room. Converting real objects to scale paper cutouts is very simple using basic math skills and a ruler.

Repeat this process with each primary piece of furniture you have or want to place in your office. If you know you'll be replacing a piece of furniture or you plan to buy a piece and don't know its specific dimensions, cut out a scale model that approximates the size of the piece you plan to purchase.

Attention Visuals! This scale drawing exercise will be right up your alley. Take the time to do it, even though it takes a little while. With your strong visual leanings, the model will make it especially easy for you to imagine and plan your new space before you purchase new furniture or begin doing any heavy work.

Laying Out Your Furniture

Experiment on paper with different configurations for your furniture and you'll undoubtedly begin seeing the difference between effective and ineffective furniture layouts. In this section, we'll look at some sample layouts and discuss some of the pros and cons of each.

Here are some criteria of effective office layout:

- The furnishings are in proportion to the size of the room.
- There is plenty of room for walking between furniture. I recommend a minimum of 22" for traffic paths.
- The primary office chair has plenty of room to swivel and roll forward and backward. A good rule of thumb is a minimum of 18" between the back of the chair and the wall.
- Computer equipment, peripherals, and other machines are easily accessible from your seated position, without requiring you to reach or stretch.
- All doors should be clear of obstructions.
- You can walk straight into the room without running into anything or having to quickly turn to avoid a piece of furniture.
- Traffic patterns between frequently used items are short and straight whenever possible.
- Seating configuration creates comfortable conversation areas.

Figure 3.5 shows an office with an L-shaped desk, credenza, lateral file, small table, and two side chairs. In this illustration, the desk faces the large window.

FIGURE 3.5

Facing directly out a window is appealing at first glance, but sitting with your back to the door can be unsettling for many people.

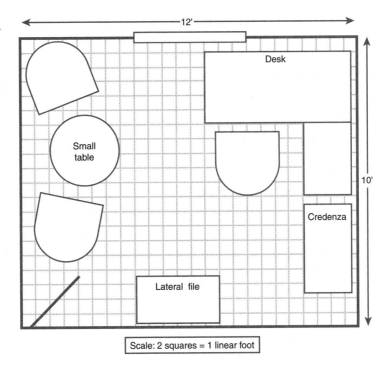

Scale: 2 squares = 1 linear foot

Initially it might seem like a great idea to have the desk set up so you can look outside all day, as in the preceding example. That would be a wonderful way to increase the enjoyment of the space. Several flaws exist in this layout, however:

- The position of the desk and chair puts your back to the door, which is a physically and psychologically weak position. When you can't see the door, visitors can easily enter your room and startle you. This vulnerability can create a subtle, underlying uneasiness that affects your focus.

- The guest chairs and small table inhibit an easy traffic flow upon entering the office.

- The position of the guest chairs and small table make it virtually impossible to use both chairs.

- The credenza in this position also creates a virtually unusable dead corner to its right, where clutter is likely to accumulate.

- The lateral file is too close to the door. It inhibits movement as you enter the office.

Figure 3.6 shows the same office space as Figure 3.5, with all the same furnishings. This time the desk is facing the door, which is a better working position. Several things are still wrong with this layout:

- The credenza and the lateral file are both behind the desk. This placement creates a very narrow walkway for anyone wanting to get to the desk and cramps the mobility of the office chair.

- The lateral file drawers will be difficult to open all the way because the file cabinet is too close to the chair.

- The guest chair is too close to the wall beside it, restricting movement.

- The traffic flow in this office is impeded. Every path you follow leads to a dead end. The closed end of each traffic path is unsettling. Many people will often avoid a space rather than feel trapped with only one way out.

- As you enter this room, you nearly walk into the guest chair to the right of the door. It is too close to the natural traffic pattern.

- The room is unbalanced. It feels "heavy" on the right side of the room and there is nothing to meet your eye as you walk through the door.

- The large empty space on the left is completely unused, making it a likely place for clutter to accumulate.

FIGURE 3.6

This layout is unbalanced with all the furniture on one side of the room, leaving little space for a comfortable traffic pattern.

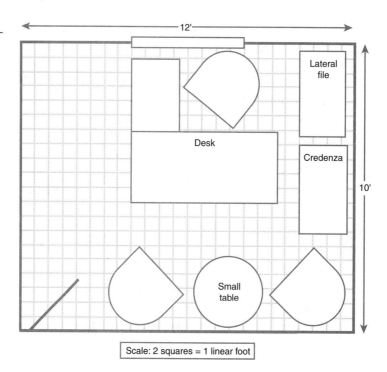

Scale: 2 squares = 1 linear foot

In Figure 3.7, the same space is configured differently, with the desk facing the corner of the office and the other furniture spaced fairly evenly about the room.

Although this layout is slightly better than in Figures 3.5 and 3.6, there are still flaws to be noted. See if you can identify the problems with this layout for yourself before looking at the list following the figure.

FIGURE 3.7
See if you can find the five problems present in this office layout.

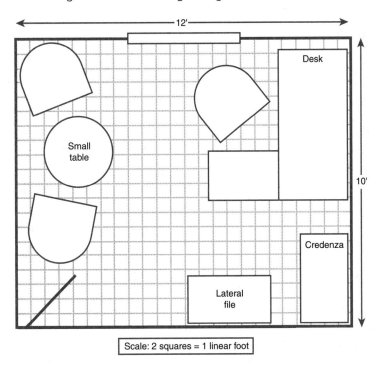

Scale: 2 squares = 1 linear foot

Here are the problems with this office organization:

- The door swings and hits one of the guest chairs.
- The lateral file and the credenza being at right angles to each other creates an odd "dead space" between them when the furniture is not being used.
- The lateral file being positioned so close to the front of the credenza makes it difficult to open the credenza doors.
- The position of the desk in relation to the lateral file and credenza forces you to walk in an awkward half-circle pattern to access either piece of furniture.
- The window at your back will likely cause a sun glare on your computer monitor, regardless of where on the desk it is located.

Now that we've addressed a few ineffective ways to arrange your furniture, let's look at the same space configured effectively, below in Figure 3.8.

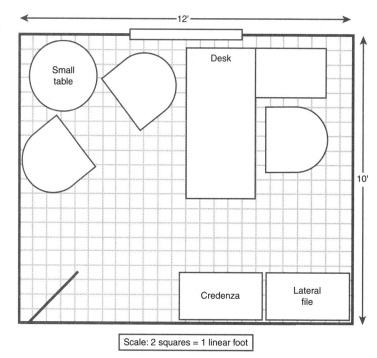

Scale: 2 squares = 1 linear foot

Figure 3.8 illustrates how, using the same amount of floor space and the same furniture as shown in earlier examples, you can create an effective office layout. The reasons this plan works are as follows:

- The desk is far enough away from the door to offer an unobstructed view of whoever comes into the office.
- The desk is situated so you not only have a perfect view of the door, but you also have an easy view outdoors, which adds to your enjoyment of the space.
- The lateral file and credenza are grouped side by side on the opposite wall, offering easy, direct access to both pieces. This configuration offers not only a consolidated footprint, but also a large flat work surface for storing Zone Two items or projects.
- The small table and guest chairs are placed so they are out of the way, but still facilitate conversation. It is easy for guests to interact with the person behind the desk.
- The furniture is arranged so there is space to walk comfortably between all the pieces without bumping your hips or knees. The room feels larger with this much free space between pieces.
- There is plenty of space in front of the lateral file to allow the file drawers to open easily without hitting anything.

- The front of the credenza is completely accessible, making it a good place to store Zone Two items.
- The office chair has plenty of room to be pushed back and swivel around behind the desk and it is just a few steps to either the lateral file or the credenza.
- The desk is positioned so even though it is in front of the window, the sun will never be over your shoulder, placing a glare on the screen.

The previous illustrations have shown you what a big difference furniture placement can make in a room. You can see how an office can feel cramped, small, and uncomfortable based completely on the furniture layout. On the other hand, you've also learned how that same office can feel spacious and comfortable simply by arranging the furnishings to create balance and logical traffic patterns.

caution When placing peripherals such as printers, fax machines, scanners and such, be aware of your health and safety. Be sure that the furniture holding the equipment is sturdy enough to support its weight, and is positioned to avoid excessive bending, twisting, and leaning backward while seated.

To do list

- ☐ Consider the impact of color and lighting on your working style
- ☐ Choose a color scheme that fits your style and your profession

Choosing the Right Colors For Your Office

If you work for yourself or you work for a company that encourages and permits you to personalize your office, good for you! You'll have more freedom as you go through this process, and ultimately, you'll be able to create a space you love because of the latitude you're given regarding your office décor.

Color and lighting can have a direct affect on how you feel, your mental state, and your productivity. A color you might use in your kitchen, perhaps a bright yellow, might not be the best color for your office because it could be too visually stimulating, making it difficult to focus and concentrate. When choosing paint colors and décor, begin by imagining how you want your office to feel when you enter it. You also need to consider what you do for a living when choosing a color scheme. In this section of the chapter, you learn how to experiment with a variety of color schemes to find the one that best matches your personal preferences and professional style.

Things You'll Need

- ❑   Paint chips
- ❑   Paint and painting supplies

Understanding the Importance of Color and Lighting

If you are an artist or you work in a creative field such as graphic design or fashion design, you might want a space that is bright, cheerful, and inspires your creativity. If you have a lot of flexibility in creating your office décor, you could also opt to go with a specific décor theme, such as Asian, French Country, or even something super modern, combining stark black, gray, and white with brightly colored accents and white metals.

On the other hand, if you work in a historically more conservative industry, such as finance, accounting, law, or medicine, where clients come into your office, you should consider using a more traditional color and décor scheme. Neutrals such as gray, tan, white, black, and navy are a good place to begin. After you've chosen your neutral, add a complementary second color to the scheme and a third accent color to tie it all together.

Before you commit to a color scheme in your head, go to a paint store and pick up a lot of paint chips. Choose more than you think you'll ever need, and don't limit yourself to a narrow range of color choices. It's better to start with more color options than fewer; almost any color can look great if combined with the right complementary colors. So, even if you don't really like a color family, resist the urge to leave it behind because you can always eliminate it later if you want to.

When choosing your color scheme, use your imagination. When you were a kid, your imagination was strong. You could easily dream up a fortress or city when all you had was a blanket and some couch cushions. So let's rev up that imagination again for this important project. Close your eyes and imagine you're in your office and it's painted all one color, perhaps a dark green. With your eyes still closed, tune in to how being in that dark green office makes you feel. Do you feel tired? Energized? Creative? Closed in? Because colors can create very real emotions, this imagery exercise is helpful in choosing the best colors to achieve the atmosphere you want in an office setting.

Experimenting With Color Schemes

When combining colors to make a scheme, there are a few roads to travel down, and you should consider options from each type before making a decision. Your three most basic options for an overall scheme are monochromatic, analogous, and complementary. A *monochromatic scheme* means you are using a single color, but working with various *values* (lightness or darkness) of that same color to create contrast and interest. A monochromatic color scheme is very easy for the eye to look at, and offers a sophisticated, calming, elegant look. For example, a monochromatic scheme in the brown family would have the walls painted a medium taupe, a lighter taupe on the trim with accents of rich, dark taupe in the art and accessories. A monochromatic scheme in the blue family might use pale blue walls, art, and accessories with dark blue ceiling and trim.

In contrast, the *analogous scheme* combines three colors that are adjacent to each other on the color wheel, such as blue, blue-green, and green. An analogous scheme is soothing to the eye like a monochromatic scheme; however, it is a bit more interesting than a monochromatic scheme because it offers more contrast and variety. One color is used as the dominant color, and the others are used in fairly even amounts to enhance and support the dominant color. An example of an analogous scheme would be three white walls with a blue accent wall, combined with art and accessories in colors of blue-green and green.

> **caution** Avoid combining cool colors (blues, greens, purples) with warm colors (yellows, reds, oranges) in an analogous scheme. Your room will feel more comfortable and cohesive if you stick with either all warm or all cool colors when using this scheme.

The third basic color scheme is called *complementary*, which means combining colors that are opposite each other on the color wheel, such as orange and blue or green and red. A complementary scheme creates a high contrast level in the space and causes visual tension by combining cool and warm colors in the same scheme. In this type of scheme, one color should be strongly dominant, with the secondary colors being used mainly as accent colors.

Examine your paint chips in the existing room light when the sun is up and when it is down. Light changes color, so your office will look different depending on the time of day and the light source present. No matter what color scheme you choose, monochromatic, analogous, or complementary, it has to be one you feel comfortable and at ease using.

> **note** To learn more about the color wheel, go to http://www.paintquality.com/color/ and click on Digital Color Wheel.

HIGHLIGHTING WITH TINTS

When using any color scheme, you can substitute a tint of one of your colors for white if you choose to. A tint is made by adding just a few drops of color to bright white to create an extremely pale color, which acts as a white without being quite so stark. You can also use a subtle pastel color in combination with bright white for a very clean, open look.

❏ Determine whether you can replace the flooring in your office, or can simply cover up existing flooring

❏ Consider concrete, hardwood, carpeting, or "green" flooring options for your office

❏ Choose window treatments that provide the best lighting, privacy, and appearance

Choosing Floor and Window Treatments

The flooring in your office will help shape the overall look and feel of the space. A concrete or tiled floor looks and feels industrial, carpet absorbs sound and gives a lush executive look, and wood or laminate flooring is sleek and contemporary. More and more companies are using "green" flooring, which means they are made from natural, but rapidly renewable resources such as cork, bamboo, sisal, and other natural grasses. These materials are all examples of green flooring products that are widely available for commercial use.

If you work in a cubicle, you won't have to worry about window treatments. However, if you have your own office, you might have a window. If you're lucky, your window brings in a lot of natural light and gives you a nice view outdoors. One thing to remember about windows is that they are only wonderful when you can control the light coming in. This means using some kind of treatment over the window to either partially or completely block or direct the sunlight. Window treatments also offer privacy, which is important to many people.

Considering Your Flooring Options

Concrete flooring can be stained and etched to make it very attractive and it might have the industrial, edgy look you want in your business. However, it's hard on your feet and legs if you do a good amount of standing in your work, so add soft cushiony area rugs in the spots where you sit and stand. The addition of rugs or soft mats will increase comfort as well as add texture to an industrial space. Here are some things to consider about popular flooring choices:

- **Wall-to-wall carpet** is comfortable and most commercial grades are durable and attractive. Choose a carpet with a pile that is short, tight, and level or tightly looped for the greatest durability, especially in high traffic areas.

- **Hardwood floors** are beautiful, but like most types of flooring they require maintenance to look their best over a long lifetime. Use area rugs or floor runners to add warmth to the room and protect high-traffic areas.

- **Bamboo** is an increasingly popular green flooring product. Besides being attractive, bamboo is a renewable material that grows faster and is harder than many hardwoods. It's also stain-resistant, which is terrific in a business environment. When properly cared for, a quality bamboo floor can last up to 100 years.

- **Natural cork** is a green flooring product that has been in use for hundreds of years and is experiencing a comeback with many designers. Cork, made from a layer of water-resistant cells that grow between the inner and outer barks of the tree, is lightweight, good for insulating, and resistant to rot, fire, and termites. Cork is also impermeable to gas and liquid, and it's soft, making it a more comfortable surface for those who do a lot of standing or walking at work. Cork is more expensive than wood flooring, but its many unique benefits often outweigh the additional cost.

> **tip** Carpet tiles are also a great way to have the look of custom-made commercial rugs without the expense. You can use a single color for a clean, monolithic look or vary the colors and textures of the squares to create an interesting design. Carpet tiles are easy to install and repair.

You might not have the latitude in your office to undertake such a project as replacing flooring. However, if you aren't satisfied with the way your floor looks or you think it conveys a negative image, consider covering it up. You can find inexpensive carpet remnants at any carpet store and have the store bind the edges for a nice finished look. Some remnants are very large, so if you find a sizable piece you could cover a large portion, if not all, of your office floor.

> **tip** If you presently have carpet or choose to add carpet to your office, consider buying a plastic chair mat to put under your office chair. These mats help your chair roll easily over a soft surface and are available at most office supply stores for less than $30.

Adding Window Treatments

Window treatment options range dramatically in cost. The most common treatments are either shades or blinds. A *blind* is a window treatment with rotating slats, either horizontal or vertical, which allows you to control the light by changing the slat angle. *Shades* are panels of cloth or other material that move up and down to either cover or uncover the window.

Some of the most frequently used commercial window treatments are horizontal blinds, also called Venetian blinds. The upside to using a blind is that you can control the light by rotating the slats. One notable downside to using blinds, however, is that their horizontal slats tend to catch dust and require frequent cleaning to remain dust-free. This is particularly troublesome for those who are sensitive or allergic to dust and dust mites.

A beautiful fix for the dust problem with regular blinds are sheer blinds, shown in Figure 3.9. Sheer blinds are much like regular blinds, except that the horizontal slats are made of reinforced sheer fabric and are sandwiched between two vertical lengths of sheer fabric.

FIGURE 3.9
Sheer blinds are a wonderful hybrid product in an office setting, offering the light-softening effect and beauty of sheer curtains without the bulk.

Some other options for commercial window treatments are cellular shades, vertical blinds, and opaque roller shades. Cellular shades are one of the most popular types, not only for their looks, but also because their cellular nature provides additional insulation from heat and cold. They are constructed using two layers of fabric with an open cell of fabric between that traps air and acts as an insulating layer (see Figure 3.10).

Choosing Office Lighting

The lighting in your office is an important factor when setting up your space. Many offices have overhead fluorescent lighting, while a home office is more likely to have incandescent, halogen, or both. Ideally, you should have three types of lighting in your office:

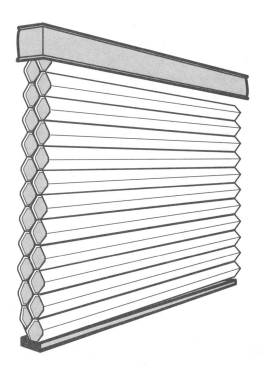

FIGURE 3.10
This side view of a cellular shade shows the insulating cell design.

- **Natural lighting** is the sunlight that comes in from windows or skylights. This light, although easier on the eyes than artificial light, can cause excessive heat and glare, so be sure to control it using adjustable window treatments. Sunlight is also the best light for viewing colors, so if you're an artist, opt for as much natural light as possible.

note If you sit in a cubicle, you won't have a window, so you'll have to work exclusively with artificial lighting. Halogen lighting is bright and as close to natural sunlight as you can get.

- **Ambient lighting** is the light that comes from overhead lighting fixtures. Ambient lighting in an office should be bright enough to allow you to easily see and work without falling asleep, but not so bright that it tires your eyes.

- **Task lighting** is focused spot-lighting used to illuminate a work surface. Task lights are fixtures that sit on the floor, on the desk, or are mounted to the wall or ceiling. Task light sources should be placed above your work surface or on the opposite side of your writing hand, to avoid your arm casting shadows on your work. If you don't have a natural light source to augment your ambient lighting or if you do a lot of work in the evenings, task lighting is especially important.

note When choosing lighting, remember that fluorescent tubes create a flicker that is nearly undetectable by the human eye, but can cause migraine headaches in those sensitive to it.

To do list

- ☐ Consider adding live plants to your office.
- ☐ Consider adding live animals to bring extra life to your office.
- ☐ Remember that plants and animals are living things and require your commitment to care for them properly.

Adding Plants and Office-Appropriate Pets

Adding plants to your office or cubicle is the quickest and simplest way to increase the energy in the room and enhance the décor. In addition, plants are excellent natural air filters, which is important. The addition of healthy, beautiful plants can give you a mental boost, too, and make your room feel more inviting and comfortable. Be sure to choose plants that are suitable for the available lighting in your office and that require only as much maintenance as you will have the time and energy to give them. Low-maintenance plants such as golden pothos, schefflera, ferns, and spathiphyllum are hearty and can generally tolerate lower light levels.

tip If you work in a cubicle, you'll be pleased to know that you can add plants to your work area without taking up precious work space. The walls of your cubicle are called partitions, and believe it or not, you can actually mount planters on them! Visit www.partition-planters.com for more information about these handy planters.

If you spend a lot of time in your office and are considering keeping a pet there, be sure you have considered the responsibilities this choice will bring and that you've thoroughly researched the animal's ability to live and thrive in an office environment. Also, be sure that your building and/or management allows such pets. An office pet requires much more maintenance than an office plant and if you travel frequently or are otherwise out of the office much of the time, it's not a good idea to house an animal there alone.

To successfully keep an animal alive and thriving at work, be sure you thoroughly research the animal's needs and do your homework before investing in any animals or equipment. Ask a veterinarian about the animal's physical and social needs. Most animals need daily watering, feeding, and exercise, and many are social creatures that require the company of other living creatures to thrive. Don't assume you can "fit" an animal into your office environment simply because you have room for a small cage, bowl, or other tiny habitat. After you have done your research, you'll be more equipped to make an informed decision about whether you can commit to the maintenance an office pet requires. The last thing you want to do is buy an office pet and end up causing it harm because you were unprepared to meet its health needs.

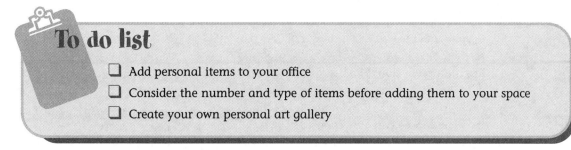

To do list

- ☐ Add personal items to your office
- ☐ Consider the number and type of items before adding them to your space
- ☐ Create your own personal art gallery

Adding Personal Items

You'll spend about a third of your life working, so your office should be a place you enjoy. To this end, I do think it's important to have personal items in the space that bring you joy and remind you of the importance of balance in your life. However, one problem with keeping an abundance of personal items in the office is that many people fail to limit themselves and their office becomes cluttered and unprofessional looking.

Personal items in your office can enhance the comfort of your space as well as give guests and clients conversation pieces upon which to build interaction with you and each other. When adding personal items to your office, it's important to be aware of the quantity you have and set space limits on yourself for those type of items. Otherwise, your personal things could take over and make it hard for you to work, focus, and be productive in the space.

A client I worked with some years ago had so many personal items in her space that she barely had a flat surface to work upon. When I visited her office, most of the clutter was a result of a large amount of photographs, figurines, souvenirs, greeting cards, and special items that reminded her of events and relationships. She said she loved having her personal things close by. She hadn't even noticed how much personal clutter was in her space, however, until I removed and boxed it up.

After we organized the framework of her office and set up organizational systems so she could better run her business, we sprinkled many of her personal things around the space to add a personal touch. We installed wall shelves that acted as a gallery to show off her photos and other memorabilia that had previously been cluttering her work space. She liked her space even more than she had before because she could fully appreciate her things now that they were on display, rather than buried on a cluttered work surface.

Projecting the Right Appearance

Keeping a large amount of personal items and memorabilia in your office can also project a less than professional image, depending on your industry. For example, those in the financial, medical, legal, accounting, or tax industry should more carefully choose the personal items they have in their offices. These are historically more conservative fields, and clients might be put off by an overabundance of personal things in the office.

Conversely, those working in fields such as art, music, theatre, retail, and design have a bit more latitude when it comes to what clients and superiors expect in the display of personal items at work. These fields are more creative and free-thinking, and clients often expect to see brighter colors, more whimsical or humorous art, and a larger quantity of fun and personal items in the space.

caution

Bear in mind that your work surfaces are for working and storing Zone One materials. If you use these important work spaces for personal items, you are robbing yourself of prime real estate.

Rather than randomly placing personal items on any flat surface, choose spots that are out of the way but still allow you to enjoy your items. Place plants on windowsills or on a table next to a window; place framed photos on the top of your desk's hutch; use the top of your credenza or lateral filing cabinet to hold sculptures or trophies; and hang diplomas, certificates, and awards in Zone Two wall space.

It's Your Style

Attention Aesthetics! You might find that your tolerance for décor is low, even for your own personal items in the space. Don't feel guilty if you only want a few family photos in your office. It's your space and it is important that you design it so you are able to focus on your work without being distracted by visual clutter.

CREATE YOUR OWN ART GALLERY

You can create an attractive "gallery" to display personal items in the office if they are too important to discard. Just like an art gallery is a collection of art gathered in a single place, your office gallery will be your own collection of important personal items, grouped together on display.

For example, hang a few attractive shelves and designate them as your personal gallery where you can display photos, awards, sculpture, or memorabilia. Because the shelf space is self-limiting and only offers so much display space, you will be forced to carefully evaluate what you choose to keep in that space, which will automatically help you avoid clutter.

Finding and Maintaining the Right Balance

Establish rules regarding how many personal items you will permit to live on your desktop. Remember that any personal items living in Zone One are taking space away from other things that could be living there instead. Make sure personal things live above or to the sides of the desktop and out of the way of your work. Personal items should be fit into your space after your functional foundation is laid. Art, photos, memorabilia, and such are like the sprinkles on a cupcake—first you frost the cupcake and *then* you add the sprinkles, and not the other way around.

Periodically ask a friend or co-worker to look at your space to check for personal clutter. It's good to get an objective viewpoint because after a while your brain stops seeing the clutter. Someone else's objective eyes will see what yours have stopped seeing long ago.

To create visual interest and keep your décor fresh, rotate various personal items into and out of your space from time to time. Good points for switching items around are the beginning of each quarter, or with each new season. Changing old items out for new ones is a good way to keep your clutter level low, while still enjoying all your things. Keeping the décor fresh will also help maintain the energy level of your office and ignite your creativity all at the same time.

Displaying personal items in your office is a wonderful way to help maintain that important balance between life and work. A comfortable, balanced office shows signs of the hobbies, travel, relationships, or interests of the person within. Remember, the goal is to create an organized space where you can enjoy being, feel successful, and be productive.

Establishing the Habit of Decluttering

In Chapter 8, "Tackling Paper," you'll learn about the value of a document retention policy. Here, let's say your company does have a solid document retention policy in place but your office is still cluttered with paper. What can you do to control it while still having what you need within easy reach? One thing you can do is to establish a habit of decluttering your space regularly. This small step will go a long way toward keeping your office organized for the long term, as well as reinforcing positive, new work habits for you.

Schedule a small chunk of time to regularly review the paper that is lurking in your office and handle it appropriately—file it, act on it, schedule action for it, discard it, or delegate it. Regularly reviewing and processing the paper in your office means you will never again have to go to the effort of sifting through mountainous heaps of paper that are months and sometimes years old.

Taking a small amount of time to declutter paper buildup on a consistent basis is more effective than taking an entire day each quarter to deal with it. Doing a little bit every day takes only a few minutes, whereas if you put it off for later, you saddle yourself with a long and arduous task you'll probably only be able to do on a weekend, when you'd rather be relaxing at home. You'll learn more specifically how to deal with paper flow in Chapter 8.

Being organized includes using your time wisely, so regularly schedule small slots of time to maintain your organization. Begin by doing weekly paper review and cleaning off your desk each Friday before leaving for the weekend. After you discover the productivity and confidence-boosting benefits of coming in to a clean, organized desk on Monday morning, you are likely to start cleaning off your desk every day before leaving work.

note New habits are often hard to get accustomed to, even if they are positive and effective, so give yourself some time to adjust. Don't assume that the new habit isn't working simply because you're finding it difficult to remember to do it or you find yourself reverting to old habits. Research shows it takes 21 days to replace an old habit with a new one. During that transitional period, you might backslide, which is normal. Don't be discouraged. Just do your best to stay focused on the positive result your new habit will make in your life.

Summary

This chapter helped you to create your office framework, taking into consideration the large concepts that contribute to an office space. These large concepts include the size of the space, the furniture in it, the layout of the furnishings, the color scheme, and the accessories and personal items you choose. You learned how to make scale drawings, as well as design an office space that is comfortable and attractive. We also briefly touched on controlling paper clutter. You will learn more about that subject in Chapter 8.

Chapter 4, "Time Management at Work," will discuss effective time management at work. This subject includes choosing a planning tool, handling interruptions, combating procrastination, and other tips on using time wisely.

Time Management at Work

The subject of time management is extensive. This chapter offers a rather broad overview of a few key time management concepts that will help you stay organized. Effective time management can only begin in your life when you realize and accept that there is no such thing as managing time. You can't manage time any more than you can manage the weather or the ocean. Time is an ever-moving, intangible resource you can't save for later or store in a box, yet it is hands down the most valuable resource you have at your disposal.

So if you can't actually manage time, what *can* you manage? The answer is that you can only manage yourself and your own actions in the midst of the passing of time. You can *allocate* time to certain tasks, which is called scheduling. You can take specific time-saving actions, but you aren't actually saving time, you're simply accomplishing those tasks in less time, thereby leaving yourself more time for other things. At the end of each day, your 24 hours is over just like mine. The only difference between you and the next guy is what you did with your 24 hours. The measure of your life will, in some ways, be counted by what you were able to accomplish in the time you were given.

To do list

- ☐ Choose a planning tool that fits your personal preferences and working style
- ☐ Learn how to get the most from any type of planner or planning tool

Choosing a Planning Tool

Deliberately planning the events of your life is one step toward getting on the road to good time management. When I say events, I don't just mean parties, vacations, business trips, and other work or social engage-
ments. Events can be anything that takes away a piece of your life, and make no mistake about it—*everything* you do takes away a piece of your life. Time management becomes tricky when you have to choose where to give away those small pieces of your life.

note Every day, you exchange a piece of your life for something. What will you choose to exchange today for?

Planning begins with choosing a tool to assist you. If you were a carpenter who wanted to build a house, you'd need a blueprint and the right tools to accomplish your goal. In your life, you can't effectively keep your entire schedule and all the details that go with it in your head and still reach your goals. You need tools to assist you so you don't waste your precious mental energy keeping track of relatively low-level thinking, such as your schedule. When you free up your mind from the burden of carrying those tasks and appointments around, it becomes more available to focus on problem-solving, being creative, and reaching your goals.

Weighing the Pros and Cons of Paper and Electronic Tools

In choosing a planning tool, you have two basic options right out of the gate—paper or electronic. So if you haven't used either one thus far, how do you choose the right style? Remember in Chapter 1, "Determining Your Work Style," we discussed work style and how it affects the way you set up and organize your office? The planner you choose will have everything to do with your personal style as well. When deciding between paper and electronic planning methods, you want to look at your natural tendencies and preferences.

Many people are very comfortable and at ease using technology, while others are slower to adopt new technological products. Some prefer the feel and speed of a computer keyboard, while others prefer the feel of a pen or pencil in their hand as it glides across the paper. But what if you aren't sure about either option? The information in the following sections can help you weigh the pros and cons of both types of planning tools, and explore which type might be best suited for your personality.

Is a Paper Planning Tool Right for You?

Paper planners come in many sizes and formats; some are pocket size while others are as large as a legal pad. There are several brands of paper planners including Franklin Covey, Day Runner, Day-Timer, and many others available at retail office supply stores and online.

The amount of space each type of planner offers for scheduling appointments, notes, memos, contact names, and task lists will be different. When choosing a paper planner, remember to consider the size of your handwriting, whether you need space for a lot of notes and memos, and if you prefer to have one page per day for appointments or if you need two pages per day. These are all important factors when purchasing a paper planning system.

Indicators that you are a more visual person who would succeed using a paper planning system include

> **tip**
> There are indicators in your personality that you can use to tell if you will be more successful with a paper or electronic planner. For example, if you tend to think of days by their date rather than their name, odds are you would prefer an electronic system. If you like to be able to review a sizable chunk of time all at once, you'd probably prefer a paper planner.

- You enjoy keeping old, historic records and reviewing them from time to time.
- You regularly keep a journal recording your thoughts, the day's events, or other parts of your life.
- The act of writing things down clarifies the thought in your mind and helps you remember it later.
- You remember where you wrote something down, whether it's on the back of an envelope, a napkin, or a business card. You might not be able to put your hands on it, but you remember where it is written.
- You remember the color of the paper something is written on, or if it was written in colored ink.
- Your thoughts and creative energies flow quickly, freely, and easily when you write with a pen and paper.
- You enjoy the various textures and patterns of paper and you like to send and appreciate receiving handwritten notes and letters.
- You often keep a stock of blank cards and stationery on hand just in case you need it.
- You make lists for everything you have to do and you often rewrite them more than once.

Attention Visuals! If you're like many visually dominant people, you would most likely prefer a paper planner largely due to the bird's-eye view it offers. Seeing a whole month in one glance is comfortable for you and makes you feel more aware of your commitments and in control of your time.

Beyond personal preferences, paper planners have their own sets of pros and cons. Here are some upsides to using a paper planning system:

- It requires no batteries, AC outlet, or special stylus tool to operate. If you can write, you're in business!

- There is no danger of it freezing up and denying you access to your calendar when you are on the road or out at a meeting.

- If you drop it, no big deal.

- You can use it as a coaster in a pinch.

Here are some of the downsides to using a paper planning system:

- There is no backup. If you lose it, you could be in a serious jam.

- Paper can become quite heavy and bulky if you carry a lot of detailed information.

- Nobody else can have easy access to your schedule, such as your boss or your assistant.

- Unless you carry a flashlight, you can't use a paper planner very well in a dimly lit meeting or anywhere else where light is a challenge.

- Searching to find past or future appointments can be difficult.

Does an Electronic Planner Fit Your Style?

Electronic planners include computer software programs such as Outlook, ACT!, Lotus Notes, Franklin Covey, and others, many that are compatible and will synchronize with personal digital assistants (PDAs). Certain personality characteristics are well-suited to using an electronic planning tool. Indicators that you would succeed using an electronic planning system include these:

- You are generally comfortable with technology and aren't afraid of trying new technologies.

- Your thoughts and creative energies flow quickly and freely when you are at the computer keyboard.

- You might remember writing a piece of information but you rarely remember where you wrote it down.

- You tend to remember appointments based upon their numbered date of the month.

- You aren't overly concerned with having a historical record of your past appointments or meetings. You're more concerned with the future.
- You love the idea of using a keyword search feature to quickly and easily find information.
- The thought of an electronic alarm to remind you of your appointments puts you at ease.

And, like paper planners, electronic planners have pros and cons that exist independent of your personality traits and preferences. Here are some of the advantages to using an electronic planning system:

- You can quickly find information by searching on a letter, name, or keyword.
- PDA units are small, lightweight, and easily portable in a purse or suit pocket.
- You can elect to set audible alarm reminders for your appointments.
- They store a great deal of information—your calendar, contacts, task lists, memos, and other information—without becoming bulky or unwieldy.
- You can use a PDA with a backlight in a dark meeting room or on a dimly lit train or plane.
- You can set passwords on the PDA, so if it is lost or stolen, it is difficult for someone else to access your information.
- Electronic planning allows others to have access to your schedule, such as assistants or superiors.
- Using infrared technology, you can easily exchange information with another PDA user, simply by "beaming" it back and forth.
- Many PDAs are robust enough to give you Internet connectivity as well as run automated sales presentations.
- Backing up your data electronically is simple and fast. Data is easy to restore from the desktop if you should lose the PDA or the battery dies, resulting in data loss.

Here are some of the downsides to these systems:

- If your battery dies or you neglect to charge the unit, you will be unable to access your information and in many cases you will lose the data.
- Electronics are subject to unexpected (and often unexplainable!) malfunctions, such as freezing up or losing data.
- Electronic planners need to be backed up regularly.

- Electronics are somewhat fragile, even by today's standards. If you drop your PDA, odds are that you'll damage it in some way.

- The display screen on a PDA is small—generally about as big as the palm of your hand—and can be hard to read.

Attention Scarlett O'Haras! If you choose an electronic planner, be absolutely sure you get a desktop charger, a car charger, or extra batteries for it. Your tendency to procrastinate will result in your letting your PDA power run low. Keep the unit on the charger or always have a spare set of batteries handy to eliminate the dead PDA problem.

Using a Combination of Paper and Electronic Planning Tools

As with your work style, which we determined in Chapter 1, you might find that the previously mentioned personality indicators also aren't completely consistent for you. For example, I use an electronic planner and I absolutely love many aspects of it. I especially love the ability to search by keyword and schedule recurring tasks automatically. However, I am also a list-maker, preferring to see an entire week's tasks on one sheet of paper, so I can cross each one off as I accomplish it. My solution is to use my planner for 99% of my planning, but I will not give up my weekly paper task list.

There is no rule that says you have to use one method exclusively, but you definitely don't want to have more than one planner for scheduling your time and appointments. Keeping two (or more!) calendars is very risky. Not only does it double your commitment to maintaining them, but I guarantee you will, at some point, forget to transfer an appointment from one to the other, which means you will end up missing that appointment. This situation could range anywhere from inconvenient to mildly embarrassing to financially devastating, depending on the nature of the missed commitment. Keeping more than one calendar is a sure way to get confused and set yourself up for time management failure.

caution Using more than one planner is dangerous. Choose *one* planner and use it consistently to track all of your time commitments, whether business, family, or social. This way, things can't slip through the cracks.

TIPS FOR SUCCESSFULLY USING YOUR PLANNING TOOL

No matter if you choose to use paper, electronic, or a combination of both types of planning tools, here are some good rules of thumb to remember:

- Choose a tool that's a size and weight that works for you. You must be able to carry it with you; a planning tool in your car or back at the office won't do you any good at a networking meeting.

- Use your planning tool to schedule every activity or task. This consistency will reduce the likelihood of missed appointments or forgotten tasks.

- Update and review your planner regularly to check for the accuracy of recurring appointments.

- Use your planner to capture notes to yourself, memos, directions, and anything else you might otherwise forget or write on a easily lost paper scrap.

- Choose a planning tool based on your personal preference and work style. Be sure it has ample room to record the information important to your work.

- Choose a planner according to the functions you need most. Avoid purchasing a more expensive planner with more functions if you won't use them.

To do list

- ☐ Minimize the time lost to human interruptions
- ☐ Handle phone interruptions efficiently
- ☐ Create a schedule for handling email

Handling Interruptions

One of the greatest productivity thieves and causes of poor time management is being distracted by interruptions. Jumping back and forth from one task to the next is not only mentally challenging, but it also hampers your ability to finish things. If you are easily distracted, take extra measures to give yourself a productive work environment. Setting boundaries—verbal, nonverbal, and physical—are all effective ways to handle interruptions of your work and take back control of your time so you can get the important things done each day.

No matter if they come in the form of co-workers, phone calls, emails, or other self-imposed distractions, interruptions are a real productivity stealer. Each time you're interrupted, your mental focus is broken, you have to shift your attention, completely change your thought stream, and *re-focus* on something new. This all takes time and energy.

It can be tempting to constantly respond to interruptions, especially if you're in the middle of a job you dislike. However, if you don't take control of the interruptions in your life, you'll find that at the end of each day you have neglected your own priorities in favor of someone else's and you have accomplished nothing, which puts you even further behind.

The stronger your boundaries are in regard to how you use your time, the more control you have. When you consistently allow people to step on your time boundaries, you neglect your own priorities and then your day ends up frenzied because you are trying to accommodate everyone else's needs first. The more you can control your time, the more you can accomplish the things that further your goals and purpose.

Things You'll Need

- ☐ Phone log
- ☐ Masking tape
- ☐ Timer

Managing Human Interrupters

There will always be those co-workers who want to stop by your desk and chat all the time, asking you about last weekend, what you're doing this weekend, or just making idle small talk. You can alleviate this problem by removing the guest chairs from your office space. If you don't offer visitors a place to sit down and get cozy, they are less likely to stay and chat for long periods of time.

Another effective technique for dealing with people dropping by and interrupting your work is to quickly stand up the moment someone enters your space. They will not feel comfortable sitting if you are standing, so they will likely not stay very long. Or, along the same lines, stand up and begin walking out of your office. Yes, I said to *leave your own office* when someone comes in and interrupts you. Invite them to talk with you as you quickly walk to the water cooler, the restroom, or the copy room. This technique will keep them out of your space and keep the conversation short. Simply and politely dismiss them *before* you get back to your desk and get back to what you were working on.

If you have a door on your office, you can always close it and post a note that says "Intense Work in Progress, *Please* Do Not Disturb." The language might seem overly dramatic, but it is out of the ordinary and lets a potential interrupter know that unless their matter is of life and death importance, they should come back to you later to discuss it.

Minimizing Phone Interruptions

The phone is a tool for you to initiate communication with others, not something you should feel compelled to answer any time it rings. Now, if one of the main purposes of your work involves you being on the phone, such as customer service or technical support, you will have to answer it as it rings and find other areas in which to limit interruptions so you can stay productive.

If your phone interrupts you constantly, turn your ringer volume way down and let your calls go to voicemail until you have a chunk of time to check and return messages. Another effective tactic is to take the call if you think it's important, but set the conversation tone from the minute you pick up the call. For example, when a person calls you who tends to be long-winded, take control like this:

You: This is Mary Smith speaking.

Jim: Hi there, Mary, it's Jim. How are you doing?

You: Hi Jim, I'm great, thanks. You just caught me and I only have 60 seconds to talk. What's up?

Jim: Oh, well, I was just reminding you to bring the sales reports with you to the meeting tomorrow morning.

You: Great, Jim, thanks for calling. I'll see you then!

By setting the expectation of a time limit right at the beginning of the call, you clearly but politely let Jim know you only had time for a very brief conversation and nothing more. Here is another effective way of setting the tone early to avoid a long phone call.

You: Hello, this is Bill Jones.

Steve: Hi, Bill, what are you up to?

You: Oh, I am right in the middle of three things. I can give you 30 seconds now or I'd be happy to call you back later. Which would be better?

Steve: I'll need a few minutes, so why don't you call me back when you're done?

You: Great. How about four o'clock?

Steve: Great, I'll talk to you then!

In this instance, you've given Steve the option of keeping the call short right now *or* talking to you later. You have clearly communicated exactly what you can offer—a short call now or a return call later. It's a win-win situation because you've set your boundaries up front, Steve gets to choose which option works best for him, and everyone comes away happy.

Attention Speed Demons! I know you love to jot names, numbers, and cryptic messages on the first thing you see. But trust me on this one. Invest a few dollars in a spiral bound phone log for writing names, numbers, and messages. Don't fool yourself into thinking that you'll remember to save that candy bar wrapper with your boss's cell phone number on it.

caution Regardless of how much you use the phone for work, it's important that you always know where to find the information that callers leave in messages or in conversations. Although scribbling down names and phone numbers on any piece of paper handy seems simple, it's ultimately a recipe for disaster because when you need to refer back to that information later, you won't be able to find it quickly, if you can find it at all!

A SIMPLE SOLUTION FOR SPEED DEMONS

Some years ago, I worked with a client I'll call Neil who was a salesman at a telecommunications company. Neil was a classic Speed Demon. He'd grab the first thing handy to record his phone conversations, messages, and numbers. He resisted changing at first, but I managed to convince him to try using a very simple phone log. It was a 99-cent spiral notebook I bought at an office supply store.

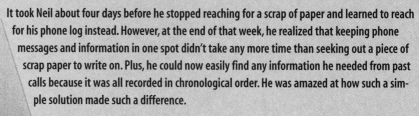

It took Neil about four days before he stopped reaching for a scrap of paper and learned to reach for his phone log instead. However, at the end of that week, he realized that keeping phone messages and information in one spot didn't take any more time than seeking out a piece of scrap paper to write on. Plus, he could now easily find any information he needed from past calls because it was all recorded in chronological order. He was amazed at how such a simple solution made such a difference.

Handling Email Interruptions

One of the biggest sources of daily interruptions is incoming email that distracts you from the task at hand. Email is simultaneously a blessing and a curse in the business world. It is an amazingly efficient way to communicate, but its tremendous convenience and ease of use has made it easily abused as well.

In fact, I have begun instructing my corporate and small business clients to put a hold on opening email for a *minimum* of 30 minutes each morning. Instead of coming to your desk and immediately firing up the email program, get out your plan for the day, choose a high-priority task, and begin working on it. Immerse yourself in catching up from the previous day before you start putting out today's fires. I truly believe that because email is so immediate, it makes everything seem urgent when in reality, very little is actually of an urgent nature.

Because we can send email so quickly and instantly, we feel pressured to react to email immediately. It shows up with a *ding ding*, and isn't it exciting? Ooooh, I've got mail! I wonder what it is? Do yourself a favor and don't even turn it on until you've gotten a good half-hour or more of work done in the morning. Being active instead of reactive will really get some good momentum going for you and will start you in a positive, powerful mindset for your day.

After you do your minimum half-hour of focused, productive work, go ahead and turn on your email program. Sift through your email, delete the spam, and respond to what you need to immediately. Then, turn the email program off or disable the new mail alert sound and get back to work on the most important tasks for your day.

By implementing the simple habit of controlled email retrieval, you will immediately gain focus and be more effective because you aren't constantly shifting your attention from one thing to the next. You don't want to be mentally jumping back and forth all day—you want to be able to cross things off your list and the only way to do that is by finishing one thing before you start another. If you have more than a few unfinished projects going at once, it might be time to change the way you apply your focus and use your time each day.

tip Train yourself to always, always, always write a name and phone number together. I can't tell you how many times I work with clients who find phone numbers written on random scraps of paper and they have absolutely *no clue* whose number it is. Take an extra second—literally one second—and write the person's name any time you record their number. When you refer back to it later, you'll be glad you invested that extra second.

tip If answering the phone is not one of your core responsibilities at work, consider covering up the message light with a piece of electrical tape during your busy work time. Covering the light will keep it from distracting you from your work.

SIMPLE TIPS AND TRICKS FOR USING TIME WISELY

As I mentioned at the beginning of this chapter, there is no way to actually save time and pull it out later to use when you need it. However, there are ways to avoid wasting it. Here is a handy list of ten easy ways to put the time you have to better use:

1. **Use every 5 minutes of every day.**

   The truth is that it's not easy to find a large chunk of time to get a big task accomplished. But if you become aware of and begin using the small chunks of time at every opportunity, you will get more done in a day than you ever dreamed possible. You will be shocked when you discover how much you can do in 2 minutes or less.

2. **Group similar activities together.**

   After you begin an activity and get into a rhythm, both mentally and physically, you can progress quicker and more efficiently. Grouping all your phone calls, all your paperwork, all your expense reporting, or all your reading into one time block will help you stay focused rather than shifting your attention from one thing to the next all day.

3. **Carve out time for maintenance each week in your calendar.**

   Maintenance is the most important thing you can do to improve your organization at work. The more you maintain on a regular basis, the less backlog you will experience.

4. **Work on what is most important first.**

   Establish in your mind and on paper what is your most important goal for the day. It will help you stay focused on that goal and resist distractions.

5. **Take control of meetings.**

   Whether you are meeting one-on-one with your boss or in a group, be sure there is an agenda in place and that it is followed. Offer to be the time-keeper if necessary and begin and end meetings on time. Nothing will kill productivity faster than the meeting that goes on forever.

6. **Save correspondence or ideas and present them all at once.**

   If you work closely with a co-worker or your assistant, resist getting up several times an hour to talk to that person. Write short notes to yourself on a single page about what you want to discuss, and then have a quick 10-minute meeting before lunch to cover everything on your list.

7. Time spent planning is time well spent.

The busier you are, the *more* time you need to spend planning your life. Establish the habit of taking a few minutes each evening before you quit work to plan the following day. Go over your schedule, your appointments, plan what materials you'll need, and write out your task list for the day. Knowing your agenda in advance will give you a good head start and allow you to hit the ground running in the morning.

8. Delegate or outsource noncore tasks.

Focus on your strengths and delegate to others what they can do faster, better, or more efficiently than you can. This frees your time to use your expertise and energy on the work that is most important to you and your company.

9. Handle decisions as quickly as possible.

Whether it is a decision about paper, a request for a meeting, or an invitation to a networking event, deciding quickly without putting the decision off for later is always the best idea. When you decide quickly, you get the item out of your head and off your plate. Delaying decisions only adds one more thing to your already full plate and you'll have to handle it at some point anyway, so why not just take care of it sooner rather than later?

10. Build flexibility into your schedule.

Allow more time than you think is necessary for each appointment or task you schedule. Inevitably, you'll run into traffic, the person you're meeting with will be late, or something else will happen that throws you off schedule. If you have built some buffer time into your day, these small crises won't ruin your schedule.

To do list

- ☐ Get to the root causes of your procrastination
- ☐ Develop strategies to break the habit of procrastination

Overcoming Procrastination

Procrastination is defined as "to postpone needlessly." The key here is the word *needlessly*. Postponing, in itself, isn't procrastination because sometimes you just aren't prepared to act and postponing is prudent action. For example, if you postpone an event because of inclement weather, it makes sense to do so. You are choosing to postpone it for a valid reason and your doing so will actually improve the event.

When you procrastinate, you put off taking action or making decisions, pretending that you'll get around to it at some unspecified time in the future. At the beginning of this chapter, we briefly discussed the reality of time as an intangible resource you can't save or hold in your hand. When you use procrastination as a time management strategy, you fool yourself into thinking that sometime in the future you'll suddenly stumble upon a secret cache of minutes that were hidden away. Somehow you convince yourself that after you find this box of time, you'll finally be able to catch up on all the things you've been putting off.

The truth is that you'll never have any more time than you have right now. As your life progresses, you might have fewer time commitments, but you'll always have the same amount of time at your disposal. So procrastination, although it seems to make sense in the pressure of the moment, only delays the inevitable.

Understanding Why You Procrastinate

Different people procrastinate for different reasons and all of us do it to one degree or another. Here are some of the many causes of procrastination:

- Fear of success
- Fear of failure
- Fear of doing something new
- Fear of change
- Fear of looking incompetent
- Poor ability to estimate the time tasks require
- Dislike of the task
- Desire for immediate gratification
- Resistance or fear of authority
- Perfectionism

For the majority of people, procrastination doesn't drastically affect their success or their quality of life. However, a small percentage of all people procrastinate on nearly everything they have to do, using it as the default method of living. No matter what the task at hand, they put it off for later. These people are called *trait procrastinators* and they live in a constant state of backlog, almost never addressing any task or challenge until it becomes an impending crisis.

Overcoming procrastination is possible for most everyone. Procrastination is simply a habit you've incorporated into your life, and it can be changed just like any other bad habit by replacing it with a new habit. The first step to changing a habit is becoming aware of when you're doing it. It is easy to know when you're putting something off because chances are you feel slightly guilty when you do it. Noticing when you procrastinate is as easy as being aware of what you are thinking and the language that is running through your head all the time.

The language that you hear constantly running in your head is called your *self-talk*. We all have it and you can't stop it from being there. It creates and fuels whatever beliefs you hold about yourself and your life. If your self-talk says you are shy, you'll be shy. If your self-talk says you're confident, you'll be confident. So taking control of your self-talk lets you change your beliefs and, therefore, change your behavior, which changes your life.

Attention Scarlett O'Haras! This section is for you! Begin to listen to and notice the words that are in your head—otherwise known as self-talk. It's these self-talk tapes that play over and over in your head that determine your success. If you have a tape playing that is negative and tells you to procrastinate, you must recognize it and change the language. When you hear your tape say, "I'll do that later," you must immediately hear it, stop the thought, and challenge that voice with something positive to break the cycle. Say something like, "No, we'll do it now so we don't have to worry about it later!" Say it aloud if you must, but the important thing is to notice the old tape, stop it as it's speaking, and replace the old thought with new and powerful language.

Strategies to Combat Procrastination

Along with noticing the language of your self-talk, there are also physical and mental strategies to help you overcome the procrastination habit. Between changing your self-talk and using a combination of both mental and physical tactics, even a long-time procrastinator can see improvement in his effectiveness.

Use these mental strategies to combat procrastination:

1. **Visualize yourself doing the task easily and quickly.** Your mind is very powerful. Close your eyes and actually see yourself easily, quickly, and happily completing whatever task you are putting off. Creating this picture in your mind prepares you to make the result happen.

2. **Vocalize to yourself as you would a friend.** Talk to yourself the way you would talk to a friend who was putting something off. If your friend were procrastinating on this task, what would you say to her? Using this technique with yourself will help you step outside of yourself and see the situation objectively.

3. **Vividly imagine the feeling you'll have when the task is done.** Use your imagination this time, not to visualize, but to imagine the feeling you'll have when the task is finished. Creating the emotional feeling of being finished will help spur you into action because you'll be motivated to have that feeling again.

4. **Negotiate a reward for yourself after the task is done.** If you are motivated by rewards, negotiate a reward for yourself after you finish the task. It can be anything that motivates you, such as a half-day at the park or

an expensive lunch. Choose something that gets you fired up as a reward to motivate yourself to receive that reward.

Here are some physical strategies that might help you combat procrastination:

1. **Gather the information or items necessary to start the task.** Sometimes people procrastinate because they simply don't have the materials or the information necessary to act or make a decision. Don't let this stop you. Take charge and gather the materials or the information you need so you can take this task off your plate.

2. **Break the task down into small, manageable pieces.** The old saying about eating an elephant applies here. How do you eat an elephant? One bite at a time! If you procrastinate on large projects, simply remind yourself that it is an elephant and break it down into bite-size pieces that are easily devoured. Use a stopwatch and set it for 15 minutes when beginning a task. Allow yourself the option of stopping after that 15 minutes are up, but realize that you might be on a roll and feel like continuing to work.

3. **Create artificial interim deadlines.** We all work better when we have a deadline looming out there in the future. If you have a long project you want to complete but your deadline is six months away, use this tactic to motivate yourself to get into action now. Set interim deadlines for yourself all along the way to keep you on task and motivated.

4. **Do either the hard or easy parts first.** There are two tactics in one here. If you are a person who likes to get the hard parts done first so you can sail through the rest of the job, do it. However, some people like to begin with the easier parts in order to build some momentum that will carry them through the hard parts. Choose whichever strategy seems to fit your personality best and give it a try.

5. **Tell others.** There is something powerful about telling someone else your goals. By sharing your goals with others, you are making yourself accountable to another person, and this in itself is motivating. You are likely to work harder for someone else than you are for yourself, so use this part of human nature to your advantage.

6. **Get an accountability buddy to work with you.** This strategy is similar to sharing your goals with another person, except this time you'll be helping someone else out at the same time. Choose a person who is also working on a similar task or project as you are and agree to keep each other accountable throughout the duration of the project. This is also a great way to make an otherwise daunting task a bit more fun, and having an accountability partner to support you is very motivating.

7. **Just keep starting where you left off.** When all else fails, just keep nibbling away at your task or project. Keep starting where you left off and even

if your results don't happen as quickly as you might want, at least you'll be making steady progress.

Every time you put something off to do later, it is crucial that you understand that there really is no later. Later never comes because at any given moment, you can only be living in "now." Therefore, anything you put off for later will ultimately end up taking place in the "now" of some future date.

Remember that nobody is perfect and almost everyone procrastinates. However, anything you can do to decrease your procrastination habit will help you be more productive and use your time more effectively. When your time management, which we know is really *self-management*, improves, the other disorganized areas of your life will automatically improve as well.

Summary

In this chapter, you learned about the importance of effective time management and planning in the organizing process. Time is your most valuable and most elusive resource, and the way you allocate it from day to day will directly determine your success and happiness.

You also learned that in order to successfully plan your day, week, and month, you'll need to choose a planner that suits your style and use it consistently. We examined both paper and electronic planning options and you determined which would be the most effective solution for you, based on your tendencies, likes, and dislikes.

This chapter also touched briefly on the subject of procrastination, which is a major factor in time management. Procrastinators are never as productive as they could be and this chapter showed you some of the causes of procrastination, as well as some real world strategies to overcome it.

In Chapter 5, "Selecting a Filing System," you'll learn how to choose a filing system that works for you so you can effectively store and retrieve your important information.

Part II

Organizing Your Files

5

Selecting a Filing System

A filing system, by its simplest definition, is merely a method of storing information so you can find it again when you need it. In other words, a filing system is really a "finding system." If you can't find information when you need it, your filing system isn't working for you and it's time to rethink the structure and method you're using. This chapter describes different kinds of filing systems and the pros and cons associated with each one. With this information, you should be able to choose a "finding system" that works best for you.

Understanding Direct Versus Indirect Access Filing

How you will access your files should be a consideration when selecting the filing system most appropriate for you and your business. There are two types of access systems: direct access and indirect access. You must decide which access method is best for you by reviewing the advantages and disadvantages of each access method.

A *direct access* system allows you to access files directly—that is, without first referring to a file index to find a specific record. Direct access is ideal for small offices or home offices, which create and store a low volume of records. Examples of direct access filing systems would be alphabetical systems or topical systems where the contents of each file are easily identified by looking at the file folder itself. If you know the file name, you can go directly to the files and access the ones you need.

In an *indirect access system*, each file is assigned an identification code that is then used to determine its location within the filing system. The identification code for each file is stored in a file index. A *file index* is simply a listing of all files, arranged alphabetically or numerically. You use the file index to determine where specific files are located within the system. An indirect access system is generally used for large-volume or complex filing systems, such as in medical or government agencies, as well as libraries. An example of an indirect filing system is a numerical system, where the name or number on the file tab gives no information about the contents of the file.

An index in a medical office, for example, would be arranged alphabetically by patient name, which would tell you the corresponding file number, as follows:

Smith, Donald F.   File Number 24883

Smith, James D.   File Number 19509

Smith, Jane R.   File Number 13440

You can also create your file index using a computer database or spreadsheet program. The computer makes it easy to sort your list by name or file number, allowing you to find the file you need in just a matter of seconds. If you have an indirect access filing system, you must accurately maintain the file index; otherwise, you won't be able to find records within the system.

If a person wants to look for a specific file in an indirect access filing system, he must either know the file code or number off hand, which is unlikely, or understand how to use the file index. Many businesses that use indirect access systems have a file clerk on staff to assist users in locating files. In addition to assisting users in finding particular files, the file clerk also often controls and restricts access to the files, increasing file security and the confidentiality of the system.

In the following sections, you learn the advantages and disadvantages of a number of direct and indirect access filing systems.

To do list

- [ ] Review the basics of using and maintaining an alphabetical filing system
- [ ] Understand the advantages and disadvantages of alphabetical filing and what type of information works well in this system

Using an Alphabetical Filing System

The Western twenty-six letter alphabet is the fundamental building block of the English language. It's not surprising that many people rely on this old familiar tool to assist them in storing and retrieving information.

The alphabetical method of filing is truly wonderful for certain kinds of information. Information that works well within an alphabetical filing system is information that is tracked by

- A person's first or last name
- A company name
- A product name
- A city
- A county

An alphabetical filing system is quite simple to set up and maintain for people who are willing to take the time to do it properly. What does *properly* mean when speaking of this kind of filing system? How hard can the alphabet be, after all?

There is some level of detail involved in maintaining an alphabetical system because there are more than just twenty-six possible spots for an item to live. Knowing that the information begins with the letter C is only the beginning of the system. Within the C block of files, there are many possible spots for any given piece of paper to be filed—or, unfortunately and all too often, misfiled.

Most people learn early and understand the concept of filing alphabetically based on the second and third letters of each keyword. For example, the names Charles, Carter, and Collins all begin with the letter C but in an alphabetical filing system, they'd be ordered as follows:

Carter

Charles

Collins

Things You'll Need

- ☐ A computer
- ☐ Filing drawers or cabinet
- ☐ A legal pad and pen

Maintaining and Using an Alphabetic System

You might think this is an extremely simple system and you're right. It is. Even the simplest system will break down if it's not used properly and consistently, however. In an alphabetical system, careful use and diligent maintenance are required to be sure information isn't misfiled and lost. For a person who isn't detail-oriented, sifting through named files to find exactly the right spot within the letter block can be torture. Such a person might be likely to simply locate the place where the letter *C* begins and stuff the file in anywhere. As you can imagine, this is a disaster in the making for the next person who tries to find poor Mr. Cochran's file.

Attention Speed Demons! If the volume of information you keep within each letter of the alphabet is relatively small, speed up storage by keeping all the A's loose inside just a few hanging folders. As your volume of paper in the A section grows, consider using only a few interior file folders to break up the A's. For example, insert a file folder labeled Aa–Af and another one labeled Ag–Am and so on until you have enough interior folders to go all the way to Az. This way you can quickly find the subfolder you need when filing information away. This method of subdividing each letter category will meet your need for speedy filing and retrieval, but still ensure that your information gets filed in the proper spot.

The type of information being filed determines whether an alphabetic system works well for the filing and retrieval of documents. An alphabetical system is only effective for information that is tracked or retrieved by some kind of name. In fact, an alphabetical system works best when filing a single type of information that is grouped together, such as clients, office locations, books by title, or employees.

Using an alphabetical method to file mixed types of information quickly becomes ineffective and confusing. Let's say you're a real estate agent and you want to file away a packet of information you received from Steve Jones, a mortgage broker who works for Centennial Mortgage Company. Centennial Mortgage is offering a new and innovative financing program for first-time home buyers. You think the program is terrific, so you want to save his information for your next young couple buying their first home. If you're using an alphabetical filing system, where do you file it?

You could put it under *M* for Mortgage Information. You might put it under *J* for Jones, *F* for Financing, or *C* for Centennial Mortgage Company. For that matter, you might even put it under *B* for Brokers. So right off the bat, you're confused because you have to make a file for it, but you have five possible choices in front of you. Let's assume you decide that using his name makes the most sense, so you choose *J* for Jones. You make a nice folder that says *Steve Jones, Centennial Mortgage* and you file it in the J section.

Fast-forward three months from now. You're working with a sharp young couple buying their first home and suddenly you remember that a while back *someone* came into your office with a terrific new financing program for first-time home buyers. You excitedly explain to them what you remember of the program and you promise you'll connect them with the mortgage company. When you go to your filing cabinet to retrieve the information, however, you have no idea who the person was, what company he works for, or how to find the information he dropped off.

Guess what? Your trusty alphabetical filing system has failed you and potentially cost you money and your reputation with these clients. The result is that you have information *stored in your system that you have no access to*, which means you might as well not have saved it at all.

Comparing Advantages and Disadvantages of Alphabetic Filing Systems

Information or items in your life that you can't access might as well not exist. Saving something for the future is only worthwhile if you put a method or system in place to find it again. If you can't find it, it's as good as nonexistent. Before you choose to use an alphabetic filing system, you need to consider the advantages and disadvantages of the system, and how well it fits with for your working style and filing needs.

Here are some advantages of alphabetical filing:

- It's a direct access system, making a file index unnecessary.
- It is very effective, provided that all users understand and adhere to the filing guidelines.
- It allows users to browse files.

And here are some disadvantages of alphabetical filing:

- Misfiles occur frequently with alphabetical filing.
- Name changes can potentially complicate both file storage and retrieval.
- It becomes inefficient in large systems.
- You must know the name of the file before accessing it.
- Unauthorized persons can easily access files.

When filing mixed types of information, an alphabetical system is more confusing than it is helpful. Opt for a topical or numeric system instead.

LOST IN THE STACKS?

If you're like many people, you save a lot of paper and, in a relatively short period of time, it becomes a big clutter and productivity problem. Did you know that you'll never refer to approximately 80% of the paper you save? The Pareto Principle, also known as the 80/20 Rule, applies to most things in life and paper clutter is no exception. You will only use, on average, about 20% of all the paper you save. However, you continue to save it because you aren't sure if you can discard it or you feel afraid to make the wrong decision. Fear-based saving is a major cause of paper clutter for many people.

You might even be one of those people who lament, "Every time I throw something away I need it the next day!" If you really examine that statement, you'll realize that your belief is exaggerated because each and every day for the past several years, you have been throwing things away that you've never needed again. The truth is that you won't need the vast majority of items you throw away over the years, but one instance in your past when you actually did might have colored your perception. Don't allow unrealistic fears to encourage you to keep so much useless paper that you can't find the documents you really need.

To do list

- [ ] Learn the basics of straight numeric, decimal, and terminal digit filing systems
- [ ] Compare the advantages and disadvantages of each system

Using a Numeric Filing System

This section will give you an overview of three types of numeric filing systems:

- Straight (consecutive number) numeric filing, in which files are numbered consecutively as they are added to the system and stored in sequential order
- Terminal digit numeric filing, which places files in order according to the last several digits in the file code
- Decimal numeric filing, which orders files topically, from general to specific, using decimal places

Because numeric filing systems are perfect for storing high volumes of paper information, they are often used in large file areas such as hospitals, banks, insurance companies, or government offices. Numeric filing is also used when the confidentiality of the information inside the files is important.

A numeric filing system is perfect for medical files because no names are displayed on the file tabs for prying eyes to look at. Patient files are stored away by patient number, date of birth, telephone number, account number, or other relevant number that can identify the patient without using his name. In a numeric system, files can also be numbered using random computer-generated numbers or sequentially assigned numbers. Numeric filing systems are mostly indirect access, requiring the use of a file index to locate records.

HIPAA (Health Insurance Portability and Accountability Act of 1996) regulations require health care providers to safeguard the privacy of their patients' information. Using a numeric system lends itself well to this government requirement. An alphabetical filing system based on patient names could potentially expose those names to unauthorized users and compromise patient privacy.

Straight Numeric (Sequential) Filing

Straight numeric filing systems simply number files consecutively starting from the first number and continuing to the highest numbered file, which is the most recent one. Files are stored in sequential order in drawers or on open shelves. It should be a pretty easy system to create and maintain, as long as you can count, right?

Although it's true that straight numeric systems are simple to use, manage, and expand because you just keep using the next number in the sequence when creating and labeling new files, they also present challenges. For example, because each file is numbered sequentially, that means the files are also filed chronologically by default. In many cases, the most recently created files are also the *most active ones* in your business. When all the active files are grouped and stored close together, it can lead to congestion in the office when storing and retrieving files.

As mentioned earlier, retrieving information from a system such as this one requires the user to know the file number in advance, or be able to find it using a file index. If your business uses computer-based billing software, you should be able to look up the purchase order number by referencing the vendor's name and checking their purchase history.

If you work alone at home or your business is small enough that you don't have filing staff to worry about, a straight numeric filing system might work just fine for you. However, if your business is already large or rapidly growing, I'd recommend you choose a different style system.

Here are some advantages of straight numeric filing:

- Straight numerical sequences are simple to use.
- Expansion is easy. New numbers can be assigned without disturbing the arrangement of existing files.
- If color-coding is used, misfiles are easy to spot.

Here are some of this system's disadvantages:

- Indirect access requires a file index to locate files.
- Files must frequently be "back shifted" to make room for new files.

Terminal Digit Filing

Terminal digit filing systems are considered by many people to be the most efficient of the numeric systems. Terminal digit systems have an advantage over straight numeric systems, but they are a bit tricky to understand at first. The core concept behind terminal digit filing is essentially simple—records are kept sectioned in physical locations based on the last digits of their file number. The file number might be the person's date of birth or a randomly generated number. In any case, in a three-digit terminal system, you group files that have the same last three numbers into sections. Then, within each section, you order the files based on the preceding digits, filing them in order. Terminal digit systems are a very effective method of filing, especially in environments where the number of files is potentially large and there is a staff to maintain the filing system. Terminal digit filing is most often used in government offices, as well as the healthcare, insurance, and banking fields.

Using a Terminal Digit System

The terminal digit system is an indirect access system, meaning that it requires you to create a file index in order to find a particular file without knowing the number. A file index is best done on a computer for easy maintenance and is simply a cross-reference document that helps you locate files. By looking up the person's last name, you can then access the file number and know where to look for her file. The terminal digit system is perfect for medical filing because it is difficult for untrained or unauthorized users to locate confidential patient files unless they know the patient's file number. It's impossible to locate a file by name unless you have access to the file index.

Some advantages of terminal digit filing include:

- Enables accurate filing.
- Allows equal distribution of new files throughout the system.
- Different file clerks can maintain different sections of the files, spreading the work equally.
- Increased file security because unauthorized users cannot access files without the file index.

Terminal digit systems have these disadvantages:

- Higher learning curve for new users.
- The index must be accurately maintained.
- Index entry is needed for every file retrieval.
- Maintaining the index can be time-consuming.

Decimal Filing

The *decimal numeric* system is perhaps the most commonly used and widely known numeric filing system. Developed in 1876 by Melvil Dewey for library use, the decimal system is based on 10 general categories. The system moves from the general to the specific, as evidenced by the major numeric groupings each being divided into 10 parts, which are then subdivided into 10 subunits. The basic framework of the actual Dewey Decimal System is shown here:

000s	General Knowledge (reference books)
100s	Psychology and Philosophy
200s	Religion and Mythology
300s	Social Sciences
400s	Languages
500s	Natural Sciences
600s	Applied Sciences
700s	Fine Arts and Recreation
800s	Literature
900s	History and Geography

The system further breaks down each of the 10 groups into 10 subsections that pertain to a different subject within its group. For example, in the group numbered 600, which is Applied Sciences, there are 10 subdivisions numbered 610 through 690, which are then broken down into 10 subsections. Each subsection numbered 601 through 699 also gets subdivided with a number as well, further breaking down each category. For example, the category 612, Human Physiology, can be made even more specific by adding more digits after the decimal point to illustrate numerical order.

> **tip**
>
> When using a numerical filing system, an important piece to remember is that in order for a filing system to work, every person who uses it must understand how it works and how to maintain its integrity. This is to ensure that records don't become lost within the system. The comprehension of the system by its users, along with a properly maintained file index, is crucial to the success of a decimal filing system.

Similar decimal system filing can be done in an office setting by substituting your own categories for the ones Dewey used. This system is an old system that was used by government and large corporations in the early part of the industrial revolution. Throughout all departments, any administrative file would be given a file number in the 100s, human resource files would be given numbers in the 200s, and so on.

Here are some advantages of decimal numeric filing:

- Very effective, provided all users understand and adhere to filing guidelines.
- Virtually unlimited expansion of files due to fine divisions within each major code.
- Rapid retrieval of information.
- All related records are grouped together.
- Unauthorized persons cannot easily access files.

Decimal numeric filing has these disadvantages:

- Inflexible and limited to 10 general classification areas.
- Requires creation and maintenance of a file index.
- Can have a steep learning curve for some users.

To do list

- ☐ Understand how topical filing systems are used
- ☐ Determine primary classes
- ☐ Set up categories and subcategories
- ☐ Compare advantages and disadvantages of using a topical filing system

Setting Up and Using a Topical Filing System

Topical filing systems are quite effective when users request information by subject, rather than by a person's or company's name. Related information on a particular subject is grouped together in the same physical space, making it simple to find information as long as the user knows the subject matter for which to look.

A topical filing system is very effective in a home-based business, a small business, or a department where only a few people access the files. Topical systems are also effective in environments where the volume of files isn't overly large and the subject matters aren't complex or intricate.

Set up properly, a topical filing system breaks down all information into broad categories or topics—"vegetables," for example—divides each topic into categories based on type, and then divides each category into subcategories. This method of filing leads the user from general information to specific information. This type of system tends to be easy to understand and intuitive for most people. An example of a topical filing system index would look like this:

caution In a work environment where the volume of files is significant, a topical filing system can eventually become unmanageable if it's not carefully monitored. When the system gets too large, some users won't understand the differences between the topics and over time topics can evolve, becoming vague or overlapping.

        Vegetables (Primary class)
            Beans (Category)
                Black beans (Subcategory)
                Chickpeas
                Green beans
            Peppers (Category)
                Bell peppers (Subcategory)
                Cayenne peppers
                Chili peppers
            Root Vegetables (Category)
                Beets (Subcategory)
                Carrots
                Radishes

Things You'll Need

- [ ]   A pencil or pen
- [ ]   Index cards or sticky notes for writing topics

Determining Your Primary Classes

A good general rule of thumb when setting up a topical system is to identify several very broad categories, which you'll think of as "departments," much like you'd find in a grocery store. A grocery store is the perfect example of how using broad "file departments" makes retrieving information simple. We'll call these broad topics your *primary classes*.

If you were to go into any grocery store—even one you've never been in before—and you needed apples, milk, and bread, how would you find those items? First, you'd think of the department in which each one would be living. You'd head to the produce department first, and once there, you'd scan the bins for apples. Next, you'd go to the dairy department and find the milk, and finally you'd locate the bakery department and get the bread.

The fact that the store is broken up into departments makes it very simple for you to quickly navigate and find what you need, even though you might never have set foot in that particular store before. The framework is such that even someone brand new to the store can find apples, milk, and bread, as long as they know in what department to begin looking.

Creating departments within your topical filing system will lead you and other users to the desired information quickly and easily. Identifying the broad departments that will make up your filing system, such as Financial, Human Resources, Operations, Clients, Vendors, Sales, and Marketing, is the first step in creating an effective topical system. Write down each department as you think of it, making sure that each department is indeed a primary class and not a category of another. For instance, initially you might make Benefits its own department, but upon review of your list, you decide that Benefits is really a smaller category of Human Resources.

The goal is to make just the right number of departments—not too few and not too many. Too few departments lump multiple topics into one department, making it difficult to find the one you want. However, creating too many departments means more possible starting points than necessary, which is difficult for users.

Creating Categories and Subcategories

After you have identified your broad departments (primary classes) within each department, the next step in creating a topical filing system is breaking each department down into its second level categories. Breaking down the departments into second level categories will aid you in zeroing in on the information you seek. Just like in the grocery store, the dairy department is broken down into cheese, milk, yogurt, and other smaller categories, and your departments should be broken down as well. Your categories should be more specific than your departments, but should still be relatively general.

For example, Financial might encompass bank loans, building mortgage papers, insurance information, bank accounts, and other information related to the financial aspect of your business. Or your department name might be Human Resources and your categories could be Employee Files, Benefits, and Payroll. These three categories are still relatively general, but if you know to start at the Human Resources file department, the categories will make it easy to quickly locate what you need.

A third level subcategory is simply the next level of detail within a topical filing system. For example, you broke the primary class Human Resources down into the categories Employee Files, Benefits, and Payroll. To further break them down, you might take the category called Benefits and break it down into 401K, Health Insurance, and Workers' Compensation. The category called Benefits is general enough that it still requires further division, hence the creation of the subcategories mentioned.

After you get to third level subcategories, give serious consideration before breaking them down any further. A third level subcategory should have at least two distinct divisions to warrant creating fourth level categories.

caution The more levels you create in your filing system, the more complicated it can become and the greater the chance of users misfiling information. Keep it simple by attempting to limit the number of times you break down a category. If you need that much detail within a topic, it could be an indicator that your information might warrant being a primary class of its own.

Comparing Advantages and Disadvantages of Topical Filing

As with other types of direct-access filing systems, topical filing has both advantages and disadvantages, depending upon the quantity and type of information you need to file and the number of people who'll be using the system.

Here are some advantages of topical filing:

- Direct access system needs no index.
- Users can browse files if necessary.
- Information moves from general to specific and the system is easy to understand.
- Rapid retrieval of information, as long as the user knows the primary class.
- All related records are grouped together.
- System is intuitive and mirrors how users categorize information in their mind.

Here are some disadvantages of topical filing:

- Users can create confusing categories over time.
- If users aren't clear on categories, records can easily be misfiled.
- Topical filing becomes inefficient in large systems.
- Unauthorized persons can easily access files

To do list

- ❑ Learn the difference between electronic document management and electronic indexing systems
- ❑ Learn about the Paper Tiger and FileWISE electronic indexing systems

Using an Electronic Filing System

The term *electronic filing system* actually encompasses two concepts—electronic document management and electronic indexing. Advances in technology have increased the ease and speed with which people can communicate and create documents. Electronic file software has also made it simpler to manage those communications and documents as they are used and filed for future reference.

Electronic document management (EDM) allows you to store, track, and distribute documents electronically. By using the software to scan each individual document into the system, you capture their color, text, and graphics and may then dispose of the original documents. After a document is scanned into the system, you simply tell the software how to categorize and name the document; the software then stores the electronic document file on either a single computer's hard drive or a central server accessible to multiple users. Also, before destroying or disposing of any original documents, be sure you're aware of your company or industry's guidelines for original document retention.

> **tip**
> To research EDM options online, use your favorite search engine, such as Google or Yahoo!, and type in the words *"electronic document management."* Remember to use the quotation marks to narrow your search.

All documents have a life cycle comprised of three stages—they are created, used, and then destroyed according to a company's document retention policy, government guidelines, industry guidelines, or all three. Because an EDM system handles all three of the life cycle stages electronically, it can be a very large—but good—investment for a company interested in reducing paper storage space and costs. There are several hundred companies that manufacture this kind of software. It is generally expensive and used in large businesses.

In lieu of a comprehensive and potentially expensive EDM system, small and home-based businesses can effectively use Microsoft Office Document Imaging, which is part of Microsoft Office XP. The Microsoft Document Imaging program comprises two functions—scanning and imaging—each with its own component. The scanning component works with any scanner installed on your computer system to make your documents accessible electronically in nearly any Microsoft program, such as Excel, Word, PowerPoint, Access, Outlook, and more.

After the document is scanned, you open the imaging component of the program that enables you to view your documents on the screen. The program will also enable you to select and manipulate text, send documents by email or fax, and perform several other functions. The Microsoft Document Imaging program also has optical character recognition (OCR), which means that—rather than storing your document as an image file (a picture of the document)—it stores it as recognizable text, making it easy to search scanned documents for specific words or phrases.

The second kind of electronic filing system is actually an *electronic file indexing* system, which allows you to retain the original paper files, stored in either random or category order, and yet still find a file quickly and easily. Think of an electronic indexing system like a card catalog in a library. The card catalog system tells you exactly where to find the book you want, and an electronic indexing system does the same thing for your paper files. In an electronic indexing system, individual papers are not scanned at all, but rather retained and used as with a regular paper filing system. The indexing system merely tells you where you can find the paper file.

note **A Brief Overview of Scanners** When choosing a document scanner, know your needs first. Will you be scanning mostly documents or graphic images and photos? Will you be scanning just a few items each week or a lot of items daily? Will you be scanning single sheets or multiple sheets of paper at a time?
The world of scanners is broad and can seem complicated, but if you begin with your primary business needs in mind, it will be easy to find a scanner that will suit you well. For more information on computer and scanner technology, visit www.pcsupportadvisor.com or www.tech-forums.net.

Here are the advantages of electronic indexing:

- Simple to learn and use
- Cost-effective for most businesses
- Offers enhanced sorting capabilities
- Can be set to remind you to back up files
- Can be password protected
- Requires no ongoing creating of new folders
- Requires no naming of files whatsoever

Here are the system's disadvantages:

- Requires regular backup of data
- Depends on the reliability of the computer to work
- Requires you to search the computer first to find a file
- Requires entering each item into the system before filing it in a folder

Paper Tiger Electronic Indexing System

Paper Tiger is Kiplinger's electronic file indexing system from Monticello Corporation. It is a very simple, yet effective system of tracking where you store any piece of paper in your office. The Paper Tiger's slogan is "Find Anything in Your Office in Five Seconds Or Less...Guaranteed!" and having used the Paper Tiger system myself, I know that slogan is accurate. The way Paper Tiger works is quite simple. You set up a skeleton framework using hanging folders that are prelabeled with numbers, from one to as high as you wish to go. Your numbered file folders will be called *reference folders*, and will be used to store information you will need to refer to later.

After you've set up your empty, prenumbered hanging reference folders, you then set up a group of action folders. These folders will be labeled with action-oriented names such as To Call, To Mail, To Read, To Pay, and so on. The Paper Tiger system provides you with the preprinted labels for these folders as well. The action files will be the ones you keep in close proximity to you so you can access them easily and frequently. After you have your numbered reference folders and your labeled action folders set up, you can begin to fill your filing system with whatever paper you wish to keep.

To use Paper Tiger, you just click on the appropriate button in the software interface to create a new file. When you are first setting up the Paper Tiger software, the first numbered file available will be file number one.

In the space allotted under file number one, you just give the file a name and then in the next space, you type in as many keywords as you want that are relevant to that file. Then, you simply drop that file into the appropriate numbered folder and forget it.

Later, when you need to find information about anything in that file, you simply open the Paper Tiger software, type in any one of the keywords you used, and the software will search for any and every file that has that keyword attached to it. "But how will I remember the keywords I used?" you might ask. The answer is to create the keywords based on the most specific, intuitive language you can think of and choose words that are common-sense enough that even another user would think of them. The more specific the keywords are to the information, the easier it will be to find it later.

Paper Tiger software is simple to install, comes with a comprehensive tutorial, and in addition to making it simple to find any paper you have filed, it allows you to catalog anything in your office you can put a number on. For example, you can catalog your reference books by creating a file location called Bookshelves and listing each book by its location on the shelf. When you need to find that book, you simply type in the title and Paper Tiger will tell you where to physically find it.

You can purchase Paper Tiger at most office supply stores as well as online by going to www.thepapertiger.com. As of this writing, the single-user version for a small office or home office retails for $170 and the multiuser version to network a larger office retails for $200 per user. You have your choice of receiving it in CD form or you can download it right from the website if you don't want to wait for the company to ship it to you.

Using FileWISE

The FileWISE system was created by a company called Organize Your World and is comprised of two parts. The first is the FileWISE Instant Filing System, which is simply a product that makes filing your paper information easy. The second is the FileWISE Deluxe Software, which is the electronic indexing part of the program.

The FileWISE Instant Filing System comes with prelabeled file guides that you can use with hanging folders or without. Each file guide is named for a different file category, including orange "active" guides for your action files, and color-coded reference file guides with names such as Insurance, Clients, and Financial. The purpose of these named file guides is to prevent you from having to create all your own categories; all you have to do is find the precreated category the file belongs to and place the file behind the appropriate file guide. The CD-ROM that comes with the FileWISE Instant Filing System includes a user manual, a file index, and a label-making software utility if you don't want to hand write additional file labels. This product retails for $59.99 for the home edition and $99.99 for the business edition as of this writing.

After you have the FileWISE Instant Filing System in place, you can add additional functionality by using the FileWISE Deluxe Software. This application is used for tracking the location of not only paper documents but also electronic documents and files. The program uses a simple interface similar to the Microsoft Windows directory tree. Within the software, you create "locations," which mirror the locations in your office. For example, you can create a location called File Cabinet #1, Bookcase, or Left Desk Drawer to name a few. After you create your locations, you simply drag the preloaded and named file categories into your directory tree.

You can create shortcuts to electronic documents inside of the FileWISE Deluxe Software, too, and file them under the appropriate category. This feature allows you to do a document search within the FileWISE system; search results tell you if the document is living in your file cabinet, on your bookcase, in your desk, or somewhere on your computer hard drive. The FileWISE Deluxe Software system is simple to install, intuitive to use, and retails for $79.99 for the single-user version. There is also a networked version available for $129.99 plus $74.99 per additional user, with discounts available for multiusers. You can find FileWISE online at www.filewise.com.

caution Be aware that in any indexing software, if you use the same keywords for several files, your search results will yield several listings. Avoid using vague keywords such as *contract*, *file*, *paper*, and other unnecessary or irrelevant words. Make your keywords specific to the paper you're filing to avoid sifting through a hundred file listings after doing a keyword search.

Summary

Whichever filing system you eventually choose to use, whether it's a single system or it combines various elements of two systems, the key to effective information management, storage, and retrieval is consistency. Users must use the system the same way all the time, and it should be as simple as possible. If the system is difficult or complicated, users are not likely to keep up with it or are apt to misuse it, causing it to break down.

This chapter touched on several types of filing systems, the basics of how each works, and pros and cons of each one. You can choose to combine systems within your business, as long as everyone involved knows and understands the guidelines and proper use of the segments of the system. Electronic indexing systems are also an option when dealing with a large number of files and can simplify the filing process. Chapter 6, "Choosing Filing Storage and Supplies," will address the various options available for storing files and choosing filing supplies and accessories.

Choosing Filing Storage and Supplies

6

T he storage and retrieval of paper is one of the most pressing challenges business people face. As we discussed in Chapter 5, "Selecting a Filing System," a filing system is nothing more than a *finding system*—simply a vehicle to enable you to store a piece of paper today and find it again tomorrow. Whether you choose to file your information using an alphabetic, numeric, or topical system, the one thing you'll definitely need is somewhere to store your files, which makes filing cabinets essential. Not only that, filing cabinets also hide volumes of information that would otherwise be out and visible, creating clutter and disarray in your office. This chapter will give you an overview of various filing furniture options, as well as filing supplies and accessories to make the storage and retrieval of your information simple and effective.

In this chapter:

* Learn about file storage furniture and boxes
* Understand how and why to use hanging files
* Learn how to choose and use file folders
* Get the facts on other essential filing supplies

To do list

- [ ] Learn about filing cabinet types and styles
- [ ] Learn the benefits of open-shelf file storage
- [ ] Understand the uses of portable filing boxes

Choosing File Storage

File storage comes in a variety of forms, including traditional filing cabinets, open filing shelves, and rolling filing carts. Although most of us have had to make do with existing filing storage system in offices where we've worked, if you have the chance to design your own system, you can choose one that best suits your working style and needs.

> **note** This chapter offers several examples and illustrations of filing products, but you can see a full variety of these items by looking through an office supply catalog or visiting the site of an online office supply dealer or retailer.

Things You'll Need

- ❑ Office supply catalog
- ❑ Computer and Internet access

Choosing Filing Cabinets

The most important considerations when choosing the filing storage for your work space are how much space you have, and how much paper volume you think you'll realistically need to store. If you are reorganizing an office, you probably already have paper files stored in cabinets or on shelves, so you already know how much file storage you need. If you're starting a business from scratch, however, or moving from a commercial office into your home office, don't overbuy before you're sure of your storage needs. It's a good idea to begin by filling one filing cabinet or shelf and then evaluating whether you need to add another one.

> **tip** When you store your files, remember that when files are packed together tightly, they are difficult to access. A good rule of thumb is to fill your file storage piece about 80% full and leave 20% empty space. This empty space will allow room for movement and make it easier for you to get your hands in and out of the system when adding and retrieving files.

Most filing cabinets are constructed predominantly of wood or steel, and each material has its advantages. Wooden file cabinets typically include a combination of solid, pressed, and veneered woods. A solid wood cabinet is more durable as well as more beautiful, but more expensive than a pressed wood type. Bear in mind that wooden cabinets might be heavier than steel, and, of course, wood is not fire-resistant. Wood filing cabinets look great and are good tools for infrequent use, such as in a home office application or for office files that aren't accessed every day.

Attention Aesthetics! Your eye for beauty probably thinks wood is more attractive than steel. If you simply must forgo the more commercial look of steel for the warmer look of a wooden filing cabinet, get a good quality solid wood cabinet. It will look better and hold up longer than a pressed wood cabinet.

For frequent filing or heavy use, steel is a better choice than wood. It is more durable and it will continue to look good even after being used for several years. Steel can also be easily repainted and has the added advantage of doing double duty as a magnet board for holding messages, photos, or other office items you want close at hand.

When choosing a steel filing cabinet, it pays to spend a little extra money for a commercial grade, sturdier cabinet with a reinforced base, full extension drawers, and double-walled steel sides. Paper is tremendously heavy and after the cabinet is loaded and you've been using it for a while, you'll be glad you bought a higher-quality cabinet because it will perform better over time.

Higher-quality filing cabinets, whether of wood or steel, offer other features of which to be aware:

- Full extension drawers that make the entire drawer easily accessible
- Drawers that glide on nylon or steel ball-bearings, for easy use
- Built-in hanging folder rails
- Thumb latches on the drawer handles, to keep drawers closed
- Internal locking devices to prevent more than one drawer at a time from being open, so cabinet won't tip over
- External drawer locks, for securing confidential files
- Exterior label holders

Filing cabinets are available from a number of sources. The big box retailers, such as Office Depot, OfficeMax, and Staples, all offer a variety of filing cabinets that range in price from $40 at the very low end to as high as $800 on the high end. Specialty retailers, such as The Container Store and Hold Everything, offer very attractive filing cabinets ranging from $45 to $250. Mass-market retailers, such as Target and Wal-Mart, also offer vertical and lateral filing cabinets ranging in price from $40 to $200. Finally, there are literally hundreds of Internet retailers offering filing cabinets ranging from $30 to $1,000 or more, depending on the manufacturer and the quality of the piece.

tip

Visit your local office supply store and try out the various styles of file cabinet. Open the drawers and compare the inexpensive cabinets to the commercial grade, full extension cabinets before making your decision.

note

Look for file cabinets with *full extension* drawers. This term means that the drawer opens to expose its entire contents, including all the files at the back of the drawer.

Vertical (Standard) Filing Cabinets

A vertical filing cabinet is what most people consider a "standard" filing cabinet, as shown in Figure 6.1. Vertical cabinets are an efficient way to store information using very little floor space.

FIGURE 6.1

Standard vertical cabinets typically have two, three, four, or five drawers.

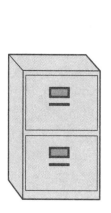
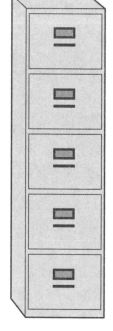

Although its small footprint means it won't take up much wall or floor space, you do need ample room to pull out the drawers of a vertical cabinet. Full extension drawers are as deep as the cabinet, so the open space in front of the cabinet will need to be as deep as the cabinet itself. You want to be sure you have enough room for the drawers to open without bumping your desk or impeding a traffic pattern.

> **tip**
>
> A two-drawer file cabinet is a handy addition to a small office because it will often fit right underneath your desk in the space that would have gone unused anyway. Be sure to measure the height and depth of the opening beneath the desk before you buy a cabinet for that space. There are no exact standard measurements for either desks or file cabinets, so you can never assume that any file cabinet you buy will fit under your desk.

Lateral Filing Cabinets

In most office spaces, lateral filing cabinets are a popular choice. A lateral file cabinet, unlike a vertical cabinet, is wider than it is tall and it has shallow drawers, as shown in Figure 6.2.

FIGURE 6.2

The tops of lateral filing cabinets offer large flat surfaces for storage or working.

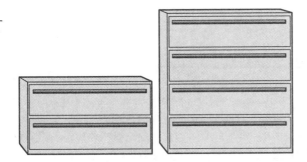

Because the drawers don't require the depth that vertical file drawers do in order to open, lateral file cabinets are a good tool for hallways or traffic areas. Lateral files are also a flexible file storage option because you can store files either horizontally across the front width of the cabinet, or you can turn the files the opposite direction, hanging them as you would in a vertical drawer, facing you, front-to-back.

tip

Some people consider hanging files an unnecessary addition in a filing system, adding bulk to each drawer. If you are inclined to avoid using hanging files, an alternative is to choose a file cabinet with high drawer sides that does not require hanging rails, but instead has an adjustable metal divider called a follower block in the drawer to keep file folders upright.

Open Filing Shelves

As their name implies, open filing shelves are open completely to the front, allowing files to be stored standing up side by side. Open filing shelves are generally used in larger companies where the volume of files stored is high.

Open filing shelves are used with end-tab file folders. These are similar to standard manila folders, but the tabs are cut into the end of the folder rather than on top. This allows the tab to stick out the front of the shelving unit so it is easily visible to users.

Open filing shelves are the most space-saving filing storage solution because they use vertical space even more effectively than vertical file cabinets do. Because open shelving is accessed from the front, files are easily stored and retrieved, even if the shelving unit is up to eight feet tall.

Open shelf filing is more flexible and versatile than vertical or lateral filing. The shelves can be much higher than standard filing cabinets because you don't need to see down into drawers, nor can open drawers create a tipping hazard. Open shelves also can be configured into mobile shelving or slide shelving, saving even more floor space. Because open shelf filing is typically used to store a high volume of records, color-coding the end-tab folders makes records access faster and easier. The topic of color-coding is also covered in Chapter 7, "Putting Your Filing System in Place."

CONVERTING TO AN OPEN SHELVING SYSTEM

If you are considering converting your files from a traditional vertical file drawer system to an open shelving system, you'll need to know how much open shelving to plan for and purchase. An easy way to figure it out is to measure your current file drawers from front to back, and then multiply that number by the number of drawers you have. The answer is the number of *linear filing inches* required.

Let's say your vertical filing cabinets are 20" front to back. If you have 10 5-drawer filing cabinets, you have fifty file drawers. Fifty file drawers multiplied by 20" equals 1,000 linear inches of files. This tells you that in order to accommodate your current files in an open shelving system, you'll need a minimum of 1,000 linear filing inches of shelving.

Mobile shelving units are a unique and efficient way of using open shelf filing to store large amounts of records without unnecessarily losing floor space. Mobile shelving units are on tracks, and can be moved back and forth to compact the units together and leave only one aisle open at any time (see Figure 6.3). Because these shelves can be extremely heavy when fully loaded, most come with mechanical or computerized options for moving the shelves.

FIGURE 6.3
By condensing empty floor space that would be aisles, mobile shelving provides almost twice the amount of shelf space as permanent shelving in the same size room.

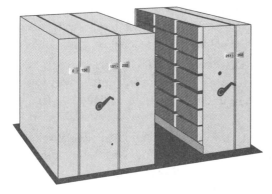

Using File Boxes

In a home office or a corporate office where each person maintains his own files, individual file boxes are an easy way to store paper files. File boxes are perhaps the simplest and most straightforward method of storing files because they require no assembly, they're lightweight, and they are portable by a single person even when fully loaded.

File boxes can be made of various materials including wicker, cardboard, recycled paper, aluminum, and metal mesh. One of the most popular styles is made of lightweight plastic and often has built-in rails for hanging folders to slide on. Plastic filing boxes are inexpensive and moisture- and pest-resistant.

Stacking filing boxes can save space and is a good solution for storing items you rarely need to access. If you want to stack filing boxes, be sure to buy sturdy models with lids. And always label the outside of the box where you'll easily be able to see its contents without opening it.

Attention Visuals! Although most file boxes come with lids, unless you're planning to put your files away for long-term storage, leave the lid off the box. You can usually just flip it over and store it upside down under the box itself. Having the box open appeals to your visual nature and keeping it near your desk makes it easy for you to see all your files at a glance.

Plastic file boxes with lids can be purchased at any office supply store, such as Office Depot, Staples, or OfficeMax for approximately $10. StacksAndStacks.com carries various styles of file boxes such as a wicker file box with lid for $35, a metal mesh box for $20, and a solid metal box with rubber feet for $35. Space Savers offers a solid wood file box with rope handles for $50 and a set of two combination wood and wicker boxes for $90. Visit them at www.SpaceSavers.com.

> **tip**
>
> A variation on the standard file box is the travel file box, which has a hinged lid that latches closed and a carrying handle. It is a great option for those who work from their cars or have to transport files from their office to home and back again. Some boxes also offer a compartment in the lid for carrying pens and other small supplies. Travel file boxes are lightweight, come in many sizes, and are available at any office supply store or mass-market retailer for between $8 and $17.

Rolling File Carts

The rolling file cart is a slightly more versatile cousin to the standard file box. Rolling file carts combine the easy file access of an open top file box with the added benefit of easy mobility. Even if you've set up filing cabinets in your office to store paper records, it can still be helpful to keep specific types of files close at hand in a rolling file cart. For example, if you work in a field where you have several projects happening at once, a rolling file cart is a great way to keep all your current project files separate from general files and have them nearby, while still keeping your desk surfaces clear.

Rolling carts are also handy in small offices where floor space is at a premium because some are designed to fit underneath a desk surface; when you aren't using them, you can roll them under the desk and out of the way. Rolling file carts are also great for storing and accessing shared files. Rather than having all the users walk to a stationary filing cabinet, users can roll the cart to the area where it's currently needed.

Attention Speed Demons! Rolling file carts are a great option for you because their open top design makes it quick and easy to store and retrieve files without ever leaving your chair.

Rolling file carts come as small as a single file box, with dimensions approximately 16" square, or they can be larger, typically 17" × 60", to accommodate many more files. Remember that although longer carts can hold more files, the combination of the heavier file load and the cart length can make the cart a bit more difficult to move and store.

Rolling file carts are available in varying price ranges (and quality), with heavier, industrial carts costing more than those designed for home office use. Rolling file carts can be purchased from Staples, Office Depot, OfficeMax, Viking Office Products, or www.StacksAndStacks.com in the ranges of $25 for the most basic, lightweight plastic cart to $250 for a substantial metal cart.

To do list

- ☐ Choose between letter or legal size systems
- ☐ Learn about specialty hanging folders for storing project and media files

Hanging Folders

Pendaflex invented the hanging folder system more than sixty years ago, and it remains one of the most widely used systems today. Hanging folders are designed to hold paper information upright by keeping it suspended and mobile. Unlike non-hanging folders that tend to slump over, curl, and look sloppy in a file drawer, hanging folders never touch the bottom of the drawer, but instead are suspended above the drawer's bottom in folders that glide across drawer rails.

Attention Visuals! Hanging folders make your filing system look more uniform, which means you'll be able to see the file you want quickly.

Letter or Legal?

Hanging folders come in both legal (8.5" × 14") and letter size (8.5" × 11"). Letter is the most frequently used size in most home and business offices, with the exception of law offices and real estate offices which historically have used legal-size files and folders. In recent years,

note Don't confuse *legal document* size with the size of a *legal pad* of paper you're familiar with. The paper on some legal pads, despite what the name might imply, is actually letter size at 8.5" × 11".

even the real estate industry has begun moving toward using letter-size documents.

If you are setting up your filing system from scratch, I recommend using letter-size file folders unless you are an attorney. Letter-size files and filing cabinets are smaller, they take up less space, are less expensive, and because most documents are letter-size anymore, it makes more sense to go with the smaller size. As we discussed earlier in this chapter, lateral filing cabinets can accommodate both letter- and legal-size folders in the same unit.

Specialty Hanging Folder Products

Within the realm of hanging folders, there are many variations in design that offer specialized benefits such as storing CDs, diskettes, and voluminous paper projects, to name a few. Some of these unique variations include

- Clear plastic hanging folders, such as Pendaflex-created EasyView, are durable and water-resistant, and enable you to easily see folder contents.

- ReadyTab hanging folders, also by Pendaflex, have a row of five built-in plastic tabs; snap up the tab in the position you want to use, slide in your label, and you're ready to go. To change the tab position, just unsnap the tab, pull it back down and lift up a different one.

- Box-bottom hanging folders have a flat expanding bottom that enables you to file more material than in standard folders (see Figure 6.4).

- Hanging file boxes, shown in Figure 6.5, are like box-bottom folders, but have closed ends to prevent items from falling out the side, either in the filing cabinet or when the file is being used or carried.

- Hanging accordion folders are similar to hanging file boxes, but are deeper and have separate sections to accommodate and categorize multiple documents associated with projects (see Figure 6.6). Hanging accordion files can be purchased at any office supply store or online retailer in the range of $8 apiece.

note To identify the contents of your hanging folders you use a plastic top tab with a file label in it. Most boxes of hanging folders will come with plastic top tabs included, but sometimes you'll find you need more tabs than are provided. Bags of tabs can be purchased at any office supply store and they normally come in quantities of 25 for about $3.

Plastic tabs are cut in different lengths, so when you are buying them, pay attention to whether you're getting the one-fifth length or the one-third length. If you tend to write large or use a label maker with large lettering, the one-third size tabs are a better choice.

note Be aware that unless you actually flatten out the bottom of box-bottom folders, they will be too tall for the hanging rails and will not fit into your file drawer very well.

FIGURE 6.4
Box-bottom folders have a flat bottom that makes the folder larger and able to accommodate more paper.

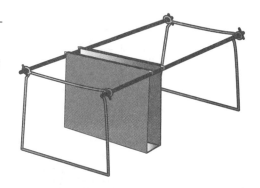

FIGURE 6.5
Closed ends on the hanging file box keep items from slipping out during transport.

- Hanging media files use the same framework as other hanging folders but are clear plastic sleeves with pockets for holding CDs, DVDs, and diskettes (see Figure 6.7).

All these filing items, although specialized, are still very similar to a standard hanging folder in that they all hang from the drawer rails, they all glide easily, and they are designed for information storage.

note Hanging media files can be purchased at most office supply stores as well as online in the range of $16 for a pack of 10 at www.ergoindemand.com or a set of 25 for $60 at www.office-organizer.com.

FIGURE 6.6
Pleated ends and divider tabs make organizing large projects easy.

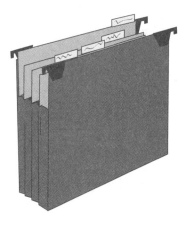

FIGURE 6.7
Clear plastic makes it easy to see the diskette or CD in the pocket of these hanging media files.

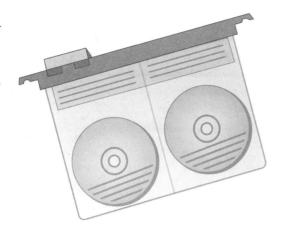

File Folders

Now that we've covered hanging folders, let's talk about file folders. These folders are typically the kind you use inside a hanging folder. As the tools get smaller, the information inside becomes more specific.

File folders are classified by their *cut,* which refers to the size of the tabs; options include straight cut (which has no tab), half-cut, one-third cut, one-fifth cut or two-fifths cut. The cut sizes refer to the width of the tab (so a one-third cut tab extends one-third the width of the folder). Folders are sold with staggered tab locations or in boxes with all tabs at the same location on the folder.

Standard height folders are tall enough that their tabs stick out above the top of the hanging folder for easy identification of their contents. In comparison, *interior* folders are shorter, so their tabs are completely contained inside the depth of a hanging folder.

note You can use folders with staggered tabs or straightline tabs. Staggering the folder tabs prevents one folder's tab from obscuring the tab of the next folder, but adding new folders can throw off the staggering order, making files harder to find. Straightline folders all have tabs in the same position, so they fall in a straight line. The human eye can identify information more quickly when moving in a straight line than when moving back and forth from left to right. Other good points about straight line filing are that it saves time when finding files, reduces eye fatigue for those who access file drawers frequently, and adding new folders doesn't disrupt the previous order of files.

Attention Aesthetics! Interior file folders are right up your alley! The tab on the folder is short enough to be concealed so all you see is a nice clean line of hanging folders.

File folders come in paper and plastic, just as hanging folders do, and it's worth it to consider the application before committing yourself to just one type. Most people use paper folders. They are made of opaque card stock and usually have tabs cut into the top or sides for labeling. Plastic folders are more durable than paper, they won't cut your skin as paper can, and they are waterproof. The best application I can think of for using plastic folders is for the files you tend to keep in sight on your desktop. If you use a clear plastic folder, you can tell at a glance what is inside of it.

caution If the thought of having your folder tabs hidden scares you into thinking, "I'll never find anything again!" you should instead opt for the standard file folders. The slightly taller folder will allow you to see the tabs above your hanging folders and although it won't look as pretty, it will put your mind at ease.

To do list

- ❑ Choose and use hanging file bins
- ❑ Understand the best uses for desktop file sorters

Other Filing Supplies and Tools

Besides the furniture and the styles of folder you choose, there are other supplies and tools available to aid you in setting up and using your filing system. We can't cover the hundreds of filing products available in this chapter, but let's take a look at some of the most available and popular items:

- Wall bins and pockets
- Desktop file sorters

Hanging Wall Bins

Sometimes you need an extra place to store files that isn't in the filing cabinet. Maybe you have projects in progress that you need frequent access to, or you might have temporary projects or files that really won't ever require a permanent home in the filing system. You can use *wall bins* to hold these kinds of files so they don't get lost and you have quick easy access to the information inside. Wall bins take advantage of vertical space—your walls, doors, and the sides of furniture—instead of the premium horizontal spaces, such as the floor and desktop.

note You learn more great ways to make the most of your office's vertical space in Chapter 11,"Using Vertical Space to Organize."

There are many different styles of wall bins available on the market but hard plastic is by far the easiest to work with and least expensive (see Figure 6.8). Plastic bins are lightweight, so they can often be installed with adhesive strips rather than screws, which is nice to prevent unnecessarily putting holes in your walls.

Some of the most popular type of bins are solid plastic and shaped like a wedge. Their triangle shape allows for storing ample amounts of paper and the large top opening makes it easy to get your hand in and out of the bin when storing and retrieving paper. The bins are also designed with a wide open top so that when you stack two or more close together on the wall, there is still plenty of room between them for your hand.

FIGURE 6.8

The angle of the top of the bin allows easy access even when they are installed close together, one above the other.

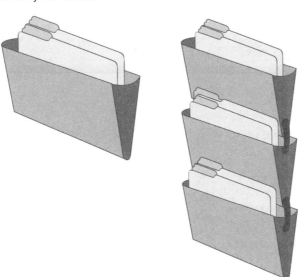

Some bins offer multiple storage slots. These attached bins can be attractive and functional, but the amount of space they consume and their configuration is fixed. If flexibility is important to you, stick with the individual bins.

The Ins and Outs of Desktop File Sorters

Your desk is a workspace, a storage space, and a place for your computer to live. Because it's the most used item in the office, your desk is also likely to be messy at times. Relax... a messy desk isn't a crime! Any area where you live or work is bound to get messy, so cut yourself some slack in that regard. It's only a worry if you can't put it back together again and things have no place to live.

For paper and files, there are many desktop accessories that will help you keep your desktop clear and functional, or at least enable you to put things back in the same spot each time! Sorters and stacking trays are some of the most important of these tools. *Vertical sorters* are desktop tools that hold your file folders standing vertically so you can keep them handy on your desktop or credenza. Vertical sorters are usually made of steel, wire, or plastic, and you can find them in a range of sizes, as shown in Figure 6.9.

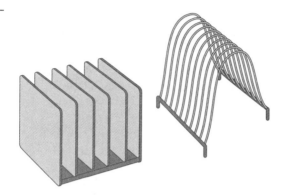

It's Your Style

Attention Visuals! Vertical sorters, step sorters, and stacking trays are perfect for you! They keep your important files out and visible, yet orderly and close at hand.

Vertical sorters are relatively inexpensive and can be found at any office supply store and many online retailers. Expect to pay in the neighborhood of $14 to $21 for a steel sorter, while the wire and plastic ones range from $6 to $10.

Step sorters are one of my favorite desktop file sorting tools. They are called step sorters

tip

Vertical sorters are good for keeping frequently accessed files close at hand on your desktop. However, I think they are even better used for items such as binders, telephone books, and other reference books. You just place the books you need close by into the sorter and turn it so you can see the spines of the books. This tool is a great way to keep books handy when you don't have a bookcase or a hutch on your desktop.

because they are designed in such a way that when more than one manila file folder is set up in the sorter, all the folder tabs are visible even though they are in front of each other. The "steps" design of the sorter raises each folder a bit higher than the one in front of it, as shown in Figure 6.10.

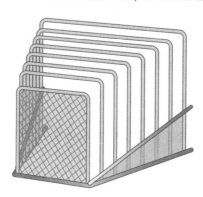

Another handy filing tool is the Oxford Decoflex hanging file holder, designed to sit on the desktop and keep hanging files close. The design is similar to the step sorters covered in the previous section. It allows the hanging files to be stair-stepped, making it easy to see each plastic folder tab. The lightweight plastic Decoflex has a footprint of just 13 inches by 6 inches, as shown in Figure 6.11. Its compact size makes it perfect for the corner of your desk, and it's available for $11 through the Office Depot catalog or online at www.officedepot.com.

FIGURE 6.11

The Decoflex keeps frequently used hanging files nearby without taking lot of desk space.

Stacking trays are a familiar tool that offers a terrific way to keep files close by but still separated by type, client name, or project. Stacking trays are simply flat trays that stack on top of each other so they don't consume a lot of surface area on your desk. They are an especially good way to store piles of identical items, such as blank forms, product catalogs, sales literature, blank letterhead, and so on.

Stacking trays are available in legal- or letter-size and come in many different styles and materials, such as hard plastic, wire, metal, and wood. Trays offering access from the side are called side-loaders and trays offering access from the front are called front-loaders.

Stacking trays vary in price and materials. The least expensive are basic, lightweight molded plastic or wire trays, available at office supply stores or online retailers for as little as $2 each to as much as $10. Metal mesh, wood, bamboo, and wicker trays have a more stylish look. Metal mesh trays typically cost between $9 and $14 per tray. Stacking trays made from natural materials, such as wood, bamboo, and wicker, range between $15 and $30 per tray.

> **caution**
>
> Stacking trays are versatile tools, but if you're not careful, they can quickly end up being black holes where paper goes to die. Be sure that whether you choose man-made or natural materials, front or side-loaders, you take the time to consider what specific information will live in those trays. Each tray should have a designated purpose and should be labeled clearly so you and others know with a glance what to expect to find there.

Summary

In this chapter you learned a lot about many of the file storage furniture options available for you. You learned how to match file storage to your office space and the file volume, and how to choose between traditional and lateral file cabinets, or open file shelves. You also learned the benefits of using file boxes and rolling file carts, and you learned how to use these versatile tools to create a filing system that matches your needs. The chapter discussed the hanging folder and file systems you can use to store documents within your filing system, and a few special filing tools to help organize your desk and office even further. In the next chapter, we talk about how to put your chosen filing system in place.

Putting Your Filing System in Place

7

Now that you've learned all you can stand about filing systems, filing cabinets, and filing supplies, you'll need to know a bit more about how to actually set up your files. Remember that a filing system is nothing more than a *finding system*—a way to store information today and find it again in the future. With this concept in mind, set up your system right the first time to avoid having to re-do it in a few months. The time it takes to set up your files properly is worth it to ensure your system will work for you. At the same time, it's important to build some flexibility into your system because as your business changes, you might need to tweak, touch up, or revamp it down the road.

In this chapter:

* Learn how to most effectively use color in your filing system
* Discover the best techniques for naming files
* Create a filing schedule that will keep you organized
* Keep your filing system flexible and up-to-date

To do list

- [ ] Learn to use color in your filing system
- [ ] Discover the pros and cons to using color
- [ ] Understand how color blocks simplify filing

Things You'll Need

- ❑ Various colored file folders
- ❑ Corresponding colored hanging folders

Using Color in Your Filing System

What comes to mind when you hear the words sky blue, sunny yellow, poppy red, or grass green? You might think of a meadow or of being outdoors. I bet you probably didn't think of file folders, did you? If you're a person who loves color, you should consider using color in your filing system. If you've chosen to set your files up using a topical system, you can use colored file folders to divide your information by category and make it simple to find the area you want quickly.

Let's say your broad categories are Clients, Financial, Administrative, Operations, and Human Resources. You choose a different color folder for each category—perhaps red for Clients, green for Financial, yellow for Administrative, blue for Operations, and purple for Human Resources. Now that your system is divided by topic as well as color, you'll find it very simple to remember where each topic is located. Creating color blocks in your filing system is also an easy way to tell if a file is misfiled in the wrong section. If a yellow Administrative file is misplaced and ends up in the red Clients section, you'll be able to tell with just a glance.

If you do choose to use color in your filing system, be sure you aren't using too many colors within the same filing area. Mixing several colors in the same drawer confuses your eye and slows down your ability to find the specific file you're looking for. By creating blocks of colored files, even if they are in the same drawer, your eye can focus on the actual content of the file labels rather than trying to pick out one color file from among several. Color blocks also allow you to know right where one kind of information ends and the next begins.

Attention Speed Demons! Color can be your friend when filing. You like to store and find things quickly, so using colored folders is one way you can identify items fast.

You can also use color when creating action files. For example, if you want to make homes for your various action files on your desk, you could use a desktop step sorter (see Chapter 6, "Choosing Filing Storage and Supplies") with different color files for each action. In such a system, People to Call could be a yellow folder, To Be Filed could be a blue folder, and Urgent Action Items could be a red folder. This is another way color can remind you of the type or relevance of the information contained inside.

COLOR REQUIRES EXTRA FILE MAINTENANCE

When you choose to use color in your filing system, remember that you are adding an additional layer of maintenance to your life. Just as you would weigh the costs and benefits of any new undertaking, you must weigh the costs and benefits of incorporating colored file folders into your office.

The maintenance involved in keeping up with a colored filing system isn't unreasonable, but it's very necessary in order to keep your system from breaking down. Successfully using color means remembering to keep a stock of all the various colors of folders you have chosen to use. More boxes of file folders means your filing supplies will eat up more of your storage space. If your storage space is super tight, keeping extra folders is a factor worth considering carefully. Maintaining a color filing system also means being committed to use the correct color for the file category when you create a new file.

If you think you would be unwilling to do the steps necessary to maintain a color filing system, you should reconsider using color at all. It's better to be realistic with yourself. If the likelihood is that you won't maintain the system, do yourself a favor and stick with a one-color system. This will help you succeed because you'll avoid your system breaking down.

To do list

☐ Learn the best techniques for hand-written labels
☐ Produce computer-generated labels
☐ Discover the benefits of using an electronic label maker

Labeling Your Files

Imagine going into a supermarket, finding the canned food aisle, and discovering that none of the cans had labels. How would you know if you were buying beans or beets? You might want corn but end up with corned beef! Now imagine your filing drawers filled with unlabeled files. How would you even begin to find the information you need or know where to store new information? Files are important to your information organizing system, but labeling your files is also a crucial aspect because it's the primary way you'll locate the information you need.

There are a few ways you can label your files, and you should consistently use whichever method you choose. Your filing system will look more uniform and pleasing to your eye if all your labels are the same style. You'll also be more inclined to keep your filing system current when you like the way it looks.

Things You'll Need

- ❑ Hanging folders
- ❑ Manila file folders
- ❑ Plastic top tabs for hanging folders
- ❑ File folder labels
- ❑ Fine point permanent marker
- ❑ Computer and word-processing application
- ❑ Electronic label maker (if appropriate)
- ❑ Pencil and paper

Hand-Written Labels

The simplest and most basic way to label your hanging folder and file folders is by using a good old-fashioned pen or marker. When labeling hanging folders, use the white card stock inserts included with the folders. Just write on the card stock, fold and tear it along the perforations, and insert it into the open end of a plastic tab. After the tab is created, just insert it into the slots at the top of your hanging folder in the appropriate spot. If you are using Pendaflex ReadyTab folders, which have the tabs already attached, all you need to do is write on the white card stock insert and slide it into whichever tab you choose, and snap the tab up into place.

When labeling your file folders, you can write directly on the folder itself, or write on white (or colored) sticky labels and then stick them onto the folder tab. If your folders are a dark color, such as blue or purple, either use a silver metallic marker to write directly on the folder tabs or use white adhesive labels. Your file labels should be easily readable from about 24", for easy retrieval of information.

tip Sharpie makes silver metallic markers for labeling directly onto dark folders. A fine-point black or colored Sharpie is best for writing on manila or light colored folders. The ink is bold and the tip is fine enough to be easy to write with, but large enough that it can be seen from 2 feet away.

One of the advantages to hand-writing your file labels is that it's so simple. You just need a marker and you're all set! If your hand-writing is sloppy or very small, however, you might find it difficult to legibly write your file labels. Also, if you're left-handed, your handwriting might have a severe slant that could make your file labels hard to read for others who might need to access your files. If your handwriting isn't suitable for creating clear, easy-to-read labels, you should consider another system for labeling your files.

Attention Speed Demons! Hand-written file labels could be a double-edge sword for you. You'll love the speedy aspect of just grabbing a pen and writing the label. However, your tendency to write quickly and not so neatly might leave you with illegible labels. If you choose to hand-write your labels, be aware that it's worth those two or three extra seconds to make your words nice and neat.

Using Computer Labels

You can create wonderful, legible labels on your computer and it's easier than you might think! Whether you use a Mac or a PC, chances are you are familiar with Microsoft Word, which is a word processing program. Word comes with a handy little feature under the Tools drop-down menu that allows you to print envelopes and labels.

Just open up a Word document and click on the Tools menu across the top of your screen. When the menu drops down, click on the Envelopes and Labels option. You'll see a window with two tabs—one is called Envelopes and the other is called Labels. Click on the Labels tab, and then on the Options button. You'll see that the options list several label manufacturers in a drop-down menu. You just choose the manufacturer of the labels you have and Word gives you many label numbers and styles to choose from.

The package your labels come in will have a style number, measurements, or both, indicating what type of label you bought. Just find the style number listed, click on its listing in Word, and then click OK. This takes you back to the prior window, where you can then click on the New Document button. Your new document will be automatically formatted so you can begin to enter text for your labels. After you're through entering the label text, insert the physical sheet of labels into your printer just as you would a piece of paper. You can print them out by clicking File, Print. That's it!

Regardless if you use Word or another word processing program, computer labels are so easy to use and give a very nice, uniform, and professional look to your files. Word processing programs are terrific for creating several labels at once, so consolidate your label-making efforts when you can. If you can bring yourself to open up Word each time, get out your sheet of labels, and go through the steps to print a new label, you'll have an attractive and easy-to-read filing system.

caution Be sure to purchase labels that are designed for the type of printer you're using. The label packaging should indicate whether the labels are appropriate for ink jet, laser, or both varieties of printer.

Attention Scarlett O'Haras! It's easy to put off making new files if you know you'll have to fire up the computer or get out an electronic label maker just to make a few new labels. To combat your put-it-off kind of style, I recommend you just hand-write your file labels. It's quick and easy and it makes filing a little faster and less painful. As you know, anything you can do to make a task seem easier, smaller, or faster means you'll be less likely to put it off for later.

Electronic Label Makers

Label makers have been around for many years. I remember as a child labeling all kinds of things around the house with our Dymo label maker. You'd turn the circular dial to indicate which letter you wanted to print and squeeze the handles together to press the letter into the colored adhesive label tape. You can still find this inexpensive manual embossing label maker on eBay as well as at other retailers.

Label makers have come a long way since the 60s and 70s. Many companies make electronic labelers and in general, they are very inexpensive and handy tools, both at home and in the office. Dymo is a major player in the labeler industry, along with Brother and Casio. All models of electronic labelers offer essentially the same basic benefit, which is the ability to create a custom self-adhesive label for files, drawers, shelves, or anything else you can possibly think of on which to stick a label.

All these companies offer varying sizes and styles of labeler, including personal and business models. Each model has its own features and benefits and your needs will determine which labeler is best for you.

Personal Labelers

Personal labelers are good tools for a small home office or for individual use around the house. Some models are small enough to be hand-held; slightly larger ones are designed to sit on a desktop, as shown in Figure 7.1. They operate on batteries or an A/C adapter and are completely self-contained, not requiring any connection to a computer or PDA. These labelers have a small keyboard and a viewing screen, which makes it easy to see what your label will look like before you print it out. They print labels using thermal technology, so there is never any ink or toner to worry with. You simply key in the letters you want, hit the Print button, and the labeler prints your new label. It's that simple! Peel the backing from the label and you're all set.

> **caution**
>
> Although the electronic labelers themselves aren't expensive, the companies that make them know that after you have one, you'll need to keep buying the label tape that goes with it. This is where they make their money. Label tapes can range in price from as low as $7 for a short length (12 feet) for the handheld machines to as much as $99 per tape for lengths up to 50 feet for the professional machines.

FIGURE 7.1

The Dymo QX50 personal labeler is available for about $30 at an office supply store.

Many personal labelers give you the option to change fonts, text size, text style, and configuration (vertical or horizontal) of the label. Generally speaking, the more you pay for a labeling machine, the more features it offers. The machines themselves run between $20 and $50, which is terrific and affordable. You can find them easily at Office Depot, Staples, OfficeMax, Wal-Mart, Target, and several online retailers. In most cases, you can also order direct from the manufacturer online if you wish.

Professional Labelers

If you need a labeler you can use every day for multiple business uses, such as printing mailing labels, name badges, postage, and labeling CDs and diskettes, a professional labeler is your best option. Both Brother and Dymo make models that connect directly to your computer and

note
Dymo web address:
www.dymo.com
Brother web address:
www.brother.com

include software so you can create several kinds of labels, all of which are printed right from the machine that sits on your desktop.

If you go to the Dymo and Brother websites, you'll see they each have a tool to help you choose the right labeler for your needs. Dymo calls it the Product Finder, while on the Brother site, it's called the Product Advisor. Each of these pages enables you to choose the functionality you need in a labeler by using check boxes. After you fill in all the check boxes, the website will automatically show you only those labelers with the features you chose. It's an easy way to confidently know which machine will best meet your needs.

These professional labeling systems are pretty sophisticated, including some that offer such features as bar code printing, as well as technology that "repairs" addresses. The address repair system automatically checks and corrects addresses by comparing ZIP codes against a United States Postal Service database. It then verifies the address, corrects any errors, and will even add the proper ZIP+4 code to the label to help ensure fast and accurate delivery of your mail.

These professional labeling systems will also print directly from standard software applications such as Microsoft Word, Excel, QuickBooks, ACT!, and others. Be sure you keep backup label tape in your office so when you run out in the middle of a project, you can continue uninterrupted.

Professional labelers are available at Office Depot, Staples, OfficeMax, online retailers, or direct from the manufacturer, and are shockingly affordable! They range from $120 at the low end to upwards of $500.

EFFECTIVE FILE NAMING

When naming files, keep in mind that your goal is to find each file as quickly and easily as possible at some point in the future. Your file naming should be consistent, regardless of what topic you're addressing. For fastest file retrieval, use nouns to name files, followed by an appropriate adjective—for example, *Health Benefits, 2005* rather than *2005 Health Benefits*. By putting the most important piece of information first (health benefits) you'll find it quicker and more easily than if you searched for the describing number (2005).

To further simplify file retrieval, avoid using cryptic abbreviations when naming files. As time goes on, abbreviations such as *MKBGT05* might be less helpful than the full spelling *Marketing Budget 2005*. The more you spell out full words, the easier your system will be to use over the long term.

To do list

- ❑ Determine how often you need to schedule filing time
- ❑ Consider investing in an assistant

Creating a Filing Schedule

A filing schedule is simply deciding how often and by what method you will maintain the storage and destruction of your information. Your schedule can be as simple or as complex as you like, and will ultimately serve you well if you apply it consistently. If you work from a home office, you'll want to give some thought to how often you want to file papers into your filing system. You can decide this by assessing how much you like or dislike the task, how quickly your filing accumulates, how easy and convenient you've made the system to maintain, and how much time you realistically have in your schedule to do maintenance.

Things You'll Need

- ❑ Container for collecting materials to be filed
- ❑ PDA or appointment calendar

Matching Your Filing Schedule to Your Work Style

You'll be filing a finite number of papers each year. Although you might not know what that number is, there is indeed a specific number. Your number will depend on a variety of factors including how paper intensive your industry or department is, how comfortable you are getting rid of information, and what your company's document retention policy dictates. For the sake of our example, let's just pretend your number is 480. Now that we know how many papers you'll need to file over the course of a year, you can choose a filing schedule that will fit into your work style.

The first thing to do is to look at your options. It stands to reason that mathematically, the more often you file, the fewer papers you'll have to file at each sitting, and the less time each sitting will require. If you file less often, you'll end up filing more papers per sitting and each sitting will take longer. It's pretty common sense stuff.

So, at the extreme end of the spectrum, if you create a filing schedule to only do filing once per year, it means you're off the hook for filing for an entire year! One of the down sides is that a year's worth of information is piling up and can potentially cause problems with retrieval. Another down side is that you'll need to have enough space in your office to store a year's worth of papers until they are filed. Yet another disadvantage to filing annually is that at some point you'll have to carve out a significant chunk of time to actually do the filing of the entire year's worth of paper. Okay, so maybe setting up a filing schedule for only once a year isn't realistic.

At the other end of the spectrum, you could try a filing schedule that dictates filing daily. On the surface, this seems like a good system because as we discussed, the more often you file, the fewer papers you have to deal with and the less time it takes. However, most people don't enjoy filing and if you pressure yourself to do something you don't enjoy every day, chances are good that it won't get done anyway and you'll end up feeling guilty about it. Unless you have an assistant who can take care of this task for you daily, it is best to avoid trying to set up a schedule to file every day.

So where is the happy medium? Find your optimum filing schedule by watching how quickly your filing piles up. Get a designated To File basket or tray and at the end of a week, notice how full the container is. If it's overflowing, you know that a weekly filing schedule is necessary to keep your filing current. If, at the end of a week, only two or three things need to be filed, let it go a second week. Check the To File container at the end of the second week; if it's full, you know to set up your filing schedule twice a month. By using this system, you'll figure out in short order how long it takes for your To File box to fill up. After you determine that, you can set up a filing schedule accordingly. Let's face it, filing isn't fun, so why do it more frequently than you have to?

Perhaps you do most of your work on the computer and you don't have many paper files at all. That's terrific news because you could file as infrequently as once a month or even once per quarter and still be fine. My business philosophy is to schedule a task—especially an unenjoyable one—as often as you need it to stay ahead of the backlog, but no more often than necessary.

Attention Scarlett O'Haras! Sometimes putting things off is okay, if it's part of your system. Don't feel guilty about putting off filing if it really isn't a necessary task. If you find you only need to file monthly or quarterly, do that, and enjoy the fact that you only have to deal with it every now and again instead of every week!

When you've determined how often you should file, schedule a time to do it in your calendar or planner. If you use a PDA or computer-based planning tool, it's easy to set up a recurring activity to remind you to do your regular filing. Be sure to allow yourself ample time when scheduling. If it realistically takes you fifteen minutes to make new files and get everything in your To Be Filed box put into the proper spot, allow twenty minutes, not ten. Remember from Chapter 4, "Time Management at Work," that the surest way to get something done is to schedule it into your calendar and then rely heavily on your calendar to guide your actions.

Getting Help with Filing Chores

At some point, your filing volume might increase, at which time you should rethink your filing schedule to determine if you need to increase the frequency of filing. You could also choose to hire some part-time help as your filing load increases.

If you're in a situation where you have a large volume of filing to do on a weekly or monthly basis and you just can't do it all, remember that delegation is an option. In a corporate setting, ask a superior or co-worker if you can share an assistant with someone else to help you with your filing. For those who are self-employed or in sales, it might be worth paying for an assistant to occasionally help you with this task.

I have a client we'll call Bill who is a Speed Demon in the business of copier sales. Making relationships and selling his products best utilize Bill's skills, talents, and energy, and he detests filing and anything else administrative. When I started working with Bill, one of the things he said gave him the biggest headache was filing and administrative tasks. He isn't good at them and he doesn't enjoy them. I suggested he delegate the administrative duties to an assistant.

He balked at first because his company didn't pay for assistants and he didn't want to spend his own money. I told Bill he would save time and make money by letting someone else do these tasks and I urged him to try it out for a month or two. What he discovered was that not only did he free up three hours per week of his time, but that the money he made in increased sales more than compensated him for the cost of paying his assistant!

> **tip** If you don't file an item immediately, write the name of the file folder where it will go in the upper-right corner. This is especially helpful if someone else does your filing for you.

Even if you just pay someone on an hourly, contract basis to come in once a week and take care of the administrative tasks, you will increase your productivity immediately. Using your precious time doing administrative work, which steals your time and your focus, can be more expensive than paying an assistant to do it. Not only that, your assistant could do those types of tasks better and quicker than you anyway, which makes delegation a worthwhile investment in your business.

> **tip** You can immediately reduce the number of papers that go into your "To File" bin by choosing to keep fewer of them. Decide if everything you have really does need to be filed, or if some of it can be tossed or shredded. The less that goes into the bin on the front end, the less that has to be filed.

Staying Flexible with Your Filing System

Very few things in life stay the same. We all change and so does business. As your business changes and grows, you'll need to be flexible with your filing system and filing schedule. Your system's structure might stay the same, even as its size changes. Be aware that all systems evolve over time; to be sure your system remains functional as it evolves, you might need to make adjustments to your system.

One such adjustment could be the way you categorize your information. For example, you might have your client accounts categorized by the state in which they are located. This system might work just fine for two or three years but in your fourth year of business, you notice that it's becoming harder to find specific files. This difficulty is a clue that your filing system might need adjusting. What used to be a hanging folder called Colorado Clients, for example, might need to expand into a hanging folder called Colorado Clients with separate hanging folders behind it, labeled Boulder, Denver, Vail, and a fourth folder labeled Other Cities.

As your filing needs continue to evolve, so will your filing system. Again, always work toward developing your system's efficiency and ease of use; when you begin having difficulties finding things within your system, you know it's time to bring it up to speed.

Summary

This chapter gave you ideas on how and when to incorporate color into your filing system, as well as a lot of information about choosing your labeling method. Whether you choose to hand-write your labels, create them on a computer, or print them with an electronic label maker, each method accomplishes the same goal of getting your files labeled so you can find what you need when you need it.

You also learned how simple it is to create a filing schedule for yourself and when to make adjustments in your filing schedule, as well as your filing system. Staying flexible with your system ensures that as your business changes over time, you'll always be able to find the information you need. This chapter completes Part II, "Organizing Your Files." In the next part of this book, you learn to organize your desk and daily work areas. You begin that process in Chapter 8, "Tackling Paper."

Part III

Organizing Your Workspace

Tackling Paper

No matter how technologically advanced we think we are, paper continues to be a burden and a necessary evil in the workplace. In addition to all of the professional mailers, publications, newspapers, and announcements we receive in the mail every day, our desks, filing cabinets, and floor space are buried under mountains of reports, memos, fact files, and other printed business materials. And the advent of email has actually generated more paper because it is so easy to instantly send a written message, and many people print them out! I hear time and time again from clients that handling their paper is the most difficult part of organizing their work lives. This chapter will help you get a handle on your paper and teach you how to keep it moving through a simple system so that it never clogs up on you again.

In this chapter:

* Learn the F.A.I.T.H. system of paper management
* Use a tickler file
* Understand how to effectively store reference materials
* Create a document retention policy

To do list

- ☐ File documents according to your schedule and system
- ☐ Act on paperwork as necessary
- ☐ Create and use an In Progress folder
- ☐ Toss nonessenital paperwork as soon as it enters your office
- ☐ Hand off paperwork to appropriate others in your office

Using the F.A.I.T.H. System of Paper Management

Acronyms are frequently used to help you remember a series of steps, names, or ideas. In managing paper, you need to have a routine system of processing information so it doesn't overwhelm you. When working with clients and teaching seminars, I use the acronym F.A.I.T.H. which stands for

- File
- Act
- In progress
- Toss
- Hand off

When you say to yourself, "I have FAITH that I can control my paper!" you bolster your self-talk, which increases your chances of success.

Suppose your office is Command Central and all paper comes through there on its way to somewhere else. By using the F.A.I.T.H. model, we can create a flow chart that shows how you deal with the paperwork that enters your office, as shown in Figure 8.1.

Things You'll Need

- ☐ A desk
- ☐ Stacking desk trays
- ☐ Desktop file sorter
- ☐ Calendar or electronic planner/PDA
- ☐ Pens and pencils
- ☐ Filing system
- ☐ Action files
- ☐ Accordion folder, wall bin, or other In Progress container
- ☐ Paper shredder
- ☐ Desk tray, basket, or other container for Hand-Off paperwork

FIGURE 8.1
When paper enters your office, it should continue through the pipeline in one of the five directions.

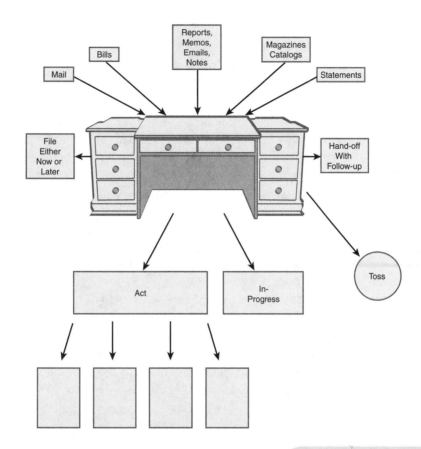

File It

The first potential path for incoming paperwork is *filing*. Anything that requires filing should immediately be filed or go into your designated To Be Filed spot. You (or an assistant) then file the paperwork according to whatever filing schedule you set up.

The File path isn't a catchall for miscellaneous documents with uncertain value or importance. Everything you file takes up space and contributes to the documents you must search through when finding the items you truly need. Only file those items you truly think you'll have a legitimate need for in the future.

> **tip**
> If you have an assistant who does your filing for you, save time by jotting in pencil at the corner of the paper where the information should be filed. For example, if it belongs in your insurance file, jot down *insurance* at the top. Or if you want her to create a new file, write *New*, and then write the file name you want it to be called.

Act

Your second path, *Act*, involves performing the recurring actions that are specific to your business. In your work life, you have a number of paper-oriented actions you repeat over and over again. To create your action files, list all those actions on a piece of paper. They might include paying bills, mailing packets, sending literature, entering information into a database, sending invoices, and other tasks.

Whatever your specific and repeated actions are, creating an action file for each one is great way to help you stay organized and on top of your tasks. Action files are simply temporary holding places for items requiring your action. They can be wicker baskets, plastic bins, or plain hanging folders, but it really doesn't matter. What matters is that you create a specific place for items to live while they await action, and that you make those files distinct from each other rather than having one large Action bin or box.

To set up your action files, choose the kind of tool you prefer, based on your taste as well as the volume of items you expect to live there. If one of your actions is reading 15 6-page reports at the end of each month, choose a tool large enough to accommodate all the reports, such as a basket, and label it "Monthly Reports to Read." If another of your actions is signing purchase orders but there are usually only a few waiting to be signed, you can use something as simple as a clipboard or a manila folder labeled "POs to Sign."

By the same token, you might find that the action file, bin, or basket you've set up just isn't adequate for your workload. What if you set up one stacking tray for invoices to pay, but your company's sales recently went through the roof and that one stacking tray is overflowing? Don't worry; just add an additional tray to hold the overflowing invoices, label it properly, and you're all set. Making adjustments to your action files should be expected, so keep your mind open for when you need to make these changes.

> **tip**
>
> Bear in mind your action files might need to be revised from time to time as your job or business changes. If you find you've set up an action file, bin, or basket called To Read and you never use it, there's no use keeping it just because it's already set up. Repurpose that file for some other action for which you might need a spot.

In Progress

The *In Progress* path is one of the most important pieces of the F.A.I.T.H. model because it is the one that keeps paper and other information and appointments from slipping through the cracks in your organizational system. The In Progress option is a designated place in which you can temporarily hold paperwork that defies classification or which doesn't fit into any of your existing action categories. In Progress candidates might be an invitation to an event in the future, plane tickets, directions to a client location, or even a birthday card, just to name a few possibilities. The In Progress file, when used properly, ensures that nothing will be forgotten or remain inactive indefinitely. Here is how it works.

Your In Progress file can be a folder, a basket, a wall bin, or a stacking tray. I prefer my In Progress file to be someplace visible and easily accessible, such as a wall bin, so it is always handy and at my fingertips. Anytime you get a piece of paper or information that doesn't fit into your action file categories or requires future action on your part, it goes into the In Progress file.

After placing the paper is in the In Progress file, make a notation in your calendar on the date you want to act on or revisit the information and mark the note with an indicator (such as *IP* in a circle) that the document is in the In Progress file. Then you can forget about the document until the date you've marked as your action date. This way, you can put something into the In Progress file in January, forget about it, and in April when it requires action, your calendar note reminds you and you can easily find the original document and act on it.

If you want to add one more level of detail to the In Progress file to make it even more efficient, you can create a numbered In Progress file and a corresponding In Progress File Index. Start by getting an expanding accordion folder with an open top that is prenumbered 1 through 31, as seen in Figure 8.2. You can then use either a lined piece of paper to pencil in an inventory of the file's contents (with slot numbers), erasing as you remove them, or laminate a sheet of paper containing a list of numbers, and use a dry-erase marker to list the file contents in the appropriate numbered lines. In either case, tape or staple the list to the front of the folder and update it as you add and remove items from the In Progress folder.

> **caution** Be careful that you don't use your In Progress file as a place to store things you don't want to make decisions about. The In Progress file is not a permanent file! It's a temporary way station for information that is on its way to someplace else.

FIGURE 8.2
This open-top expanding file is the perfect desktop sorter to use as an In Progress file.

Toss

The fourth path is *Toss*, which is my favorite one! Paring down the volume of paper in your life is the first, best, and easiest way to start getting organized. Tossing also involves evaluating paper for confidential information that would warrant its shredding instead. In Chapter 2, "Creating Your Office Vision," we touched briefly on shredding to avoid identity theft. It's important to shred any company paperwork with information on it that would compromise your clients, vendors, employees, or the security of your company itself. Any papers containing information such as account numbers, Social Security numbers, policy numbers, or proprietary information should be shredded rather than simply thrown into the trash.

If you don't have shredders or your volume of paper is high, you can hire a company to come to your business and shred your confidential material on-site. These shredding services generally charge you according to the volume of paper to shred and the shredding

> **tip** The secret to the long-term success of the In Progress file is using it in conjunction with your calendar every time. If you put paper into the In Progress file and you don't make a note to follow up on your calendar, you will inevitably forget that the paper is in there and it will live in there indefinitely.

process is quick and efficient. Most will give you a certification of destruction after the fact, guaranteeing that your confidential information was indeed shredded. Shred-It (www.shredit.com) and Iron Mountain (www.ironmountain.com) are two reputable shredding companies who can help you with your document destruction needs.

Use your trashcan and shredder freely, especially when you know you can find the information again elsewhere if you ever need to. There is no reason to keep paper you aren't required to keep and, in fact, your document retention policy might require that you immediately destroy certain kinds of paper informa-

> **tip** To learn more about document destruction, visit the National Association for Information Destruction, Inc. at their website www.naidonline.org.

tion, such as prior versions of documents or contracts. You'll learn more about creating a document retention policy at the end of this chapter.

Hand Off

The fifth and final path on the F.A.I.T.H. model is the *Hand Off*. This path is for information that doesn't belong to you, or needs to be delegated to someone else for action either before you act or in lieu of your acting on it. Hand Off enables you to separate incoming paper that needs to continue moving on to another person or department.

> **caution** As fun and exciting as tossing and shredding can be, make sure before you toss too much that you are familiar with your company's document retention policy. You definitely don't want to be destroying anything that could get you into hot water.

You might have individuals you hand off paper to regularly, in which case each person should have a designated spot where his paper lives until he comes to pick it up. If you have an assistant, it's a good idea to make a storage bin for anything you want to travel back and forth between both of you. The Hand Off bin acts as a mailbox of sorts, and any time there is something in the box, the assistant knows it requires action on her part.

If you create a Hand Off bin or basket, be sure to label it with the person's name so everyone in the office can tell who has mail. If you don't always delegate to the same person, write the person's name on a sticky note and post it to the top corner of the paper. Either deliver the paper to that person yourself or leave a message or email asking the person to come get it out of the Hand Off box.

note Anytime you delegate or hand off something that is ultimately your responsibility, make sure to put a note into your calendar to remind yourself to follow up with the person to whom you delegated. This lets them know you are still in the loop and keeps you from forgetting about the project or task.

To do list

- ☐ Learn to sort mail quickly
- ☐ Set up action files for incoming mail

Handling Incoming Mail Using the F.A.I.T.H. System

Neither rain nor snow nor dark of night will stop the postman from his appointed rounds! Well thank you very much, Mr. Postman, but would you reconsider for just a day or two? It seems we get more mail than ever and the worst part is that no matter what you do, it never stops coming! This section will help you process mail using the F.A.I.T.H. system, which you learned previously in this chapter.

Things You'll Need

- ☐ A desk
- ☐ Desk trays, bins, or baskets
- ☐ Pens and pencils

So what's the secret to staying caught up with all that incoming paper? Simply put, just like any organizing project, it's a multistep system that involves four aspects:

1. Fast, effective decision making.
2. Putting the right tools in place.
3. Establishing new habits and routines.
4. Committing time to using and maintaining the system.

Processing the mail should be a priority in your office. If your mail isn't processed regularly, it will pile up, and some of it will no doubt be time-sensitive material that requires prompt action. Whether someone else collects your business mail or you do it yourself, you'll need to have a system to sort it, toss the unimportant pieces, categorize the rest, and act on those pieces that require action.

note If you don't know or don't have the authority, yet you still have the responsibility for the mail, ask a superior or colleague to help you create a list of criteria for various types of mail, so you *can* handle that task effectively.

Setting Up a Sorting Station and System

Sorting mail is a pretty simple task as long as you have the information and the authority to make decisions about what to keep versus what to throw away. Start by creating one place in your office where incoming mail will live until it gets sorted. It could be a bin, a box, or a basket. It doesn't matter what it is, but whatever you choose, be sure it's easily accessible to the person who brings in your mail. Choose a mail container large enough to hold at least two days' worth of mail. Even if your goal is to process mail daily, there will always be times when you can't do it or you're out of town. If your mail container is plenty large enough for two days' mail, it won't overflow even if you miss a day.

Sorting mail is a two-part process: First you decide, and then you act. In fact, this two-part process is the key to keeping most things in your life from becoming backlogged. You first must decide which mail is junk mail, and then you must act immediately by throwing it away. It might sound silly, but you'd be surprised how many people pile up junk mail instead of throwing it away because they're afraid that there just might be some golden nugget in that pile they can't live without. Your life is busy enough without spending precious time opening and reading junk mail or useless catalogs. These should be tossed out before they even hit your desk. If you process mail for others, be sure to establish a criteria so you aren't unknowingly throwing out junk mail that is important to someone else.

Fast, effective decision-making is a fundamental building block of organization. If you are a slow decision maker who consistently puts off decisions for later, I guarantee you are living a cluttered and chaotic existence. Part of being an adult is learning to make decisions, acting upon them, and accepting the results. If life moves faster than your decision-making skills are moving, you will fall behind. Period.

Now that you've thrown away the junk mail, your next step is to categorize the rest—again, you must decide and act. Decide what category each piece falls into, based on the action it requires next. Some mail, such as magazines or noncritical correspondence, can be read and thrown away. Some mail, such as financial statements, must be read and filed away. Other mail, such as bills, personal correspondence, invitations, contracts, or business forms needs to be read and acted upon.

After you assess each piece, place it in the appropriate spot until you come back to it later. These designated places should be easily accessible, clearly labeled and in plain view.

Using Your Mail System

Now that you've set up your mail processing station, you're almost there, but not quite. Creating an effective system means using the appropriate tools and new habits together. Using tools without consistent habits isn't a system at all. When you consistently apply the habit of sorting, tossing, categorizing, placing your mail in the designated spots, and then acting on those decisions, you are using the *system*.

Any system you set up in your life to make routine tasks simpler and faster will require a commitment to use and maintain it. This is why it's so important to set up systems that seem easy for you to keep up with long-term. If you create a system that's complicated, chances are good you'll abandon it in short order and then you're back to square one.

> **note** Your action files for mail might be the same ones you're already using. If you've set up a To File spot, go ahead and use it for mail that needs to be filed as well. There is no sense in duplicating action files. The tools you choose for your mail sorting station can be as simple as a few letter trays, stacked up on your desktop, and clearly labeled according to their next action.

Attention Ponderers! You often fail to act because it requires you to commit to a direction or a decision. The secret to breaking yourself of the inability to act is to get comfortable with the inherent risk involved in making a decision. Becoming an organized person involves learning to make a decision based on the information you have *at the time*, and sticking with it. The more you practice something, the easier it becomes, so start by forcing yourself to make small decisions quickly, no matter how insignificant they seem. You'll see that you *can* make good decisions quickly, which will build your confidence and help you lose your fear.

To do list

- ☐ Learn about tickler files
- ☐ Understand how to set up and use a tickler file

Using a Tickler File

A tickler file, if used consistently, can be a very effective paper management system. It is called a *tickler* file because it literally "tickles" your memory about an appointment or an item you want to address or act on.

Some people make a tickler file using a file drawer, where the file is close at hand. A good space to make into a tickler is a file drawer in your desk. It's easy to create using hanging files and tabs.

To do list

- ☐ An empty file drawer
- ☐ 43 hanging folders
- ☐ 43 plastic tabs
- ☐ Label maker or marker

To create your tickler file, start by labeling 12 hanging folders, one for each month of the year. Then label the remaining 31 folders with numbers from 1 through 31 to correspond to days of the current month. Put all the folders into a Zone 1 file drawer or into a desktop hanging file, with the 1–31 current folders in front of the twelve monthly folders.

To use your tickler file, place anything that needs your attention in a future month into the folder labeled with the appropriate month. For example, if it's currently February and you have a piece of information you'd like to revisit in June, put it into the June hanging folder. Anything that requires your attention this month goes into the appropriately numbered date folder between 1 and 31. If you want to send an event registration on the tenth of this month, you'd drop the registration form into folder number 10.

You can use your tickler for paying bills, by placing the bill into the date folder corresponding to when you want to pay it. If an invoice is due on the fifteenth of this month, you place the invoice into the folder labeled the tenth to allow a five-day buffer for mailing time.

caution Any organizational system is only effective if it is used consistently. You can create the most beautiful tickler file in the world but unless you get in the habit of checking it *every single day without fail*, your system will break down rapidly. Many people who purchase or create tickler files never create the habit of checking them daily, and then they end up not using them at all.

You can also use your tickler file to remind yourself to contact clients and prospects. Simply place either the client's entire file or a handwritten note into the appropriate follow-up date or month file. When you check your tickler on that date, you'll find the reminder to follow up with that client or prospect.

USING A BOUND OR DESKTOP TICKLER FILE

Tickler files also come in the form of bound books or wooden desktop pieces with 31 slots. The bound book version is called a desktop file sorter. It is a book with tabbed pages labeled 1–31, with the month names, or both. The pages are made of heavy-duty pressboard and the spine is bound so it can expand as you add papers between the pages. Many have a large hole drilled through the center of each page to enable you to see at a glance if there is any paper in the pages beneath the current page. It's just another visual reminder for you to remember to check each day's page.

Desktop tickler files are attractive office pieces, available in wood, and they have 31 vertical slots in them. Each slot is rather slender so it won't hold things such as client files, but is better suited for paying bills or hand-written notes. Many of this type of tickler file also have small drawers beneath the vertical slots for holding stamps, envelopes, staplers, and other office supplies (see Figure 8.3). These can be bought at office supply stores or online at www.lillianvernon.com for about $40.

FIGURE 8.3

The desktop tickler file is an attractive tool for managing time-sensitive material.

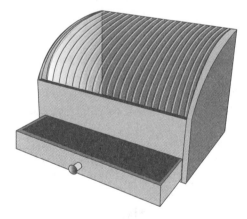

Attention Visuals! A desktop tickler file will be the better choice for you rather than one that lives inside a file drawer. You have a tendency to forget things that aren't in your sight, so having the tickler on your desktop, whether it's the bound book or the wooden piece with slots, will help keep you on top of your action items.

To do list

- ❏ Understand Zones with regard to reference materials
- ❏ Store reference materials properly

Storing Reference Materials

Reference materials, such as company directories, territory maps, charts, catalogs or user manuals, are used on a frequent and consistent basis and therefore have a longer life cycle in than most other types of office paperwork. Whatever reference materials you use in your industry, you need to be able to store them in a way that makes the information easily accessible and yet out of the way of your work.

Things You'll Need

- ❏ Reference materials
- ❏ Magazine boxes
- ❏ Three-ring binders

Essentially, reference materials are no different than any other item in your office. Although they are relevant and necessary, you must decide where to store them based on their frequency of use. To do so, you can use the office Zone system we discussed for storing office supplies, computer equipment, and so on in Chapter 2. In that plan, the zone nearest your desk is Zone One, the next most accessible area is Zone Two, and so on. In this system, charts and tables you refer to daily, for example, belong in Zone One, where you can quickly access them. A company directory you really need to keep, yet only access once or twice a quarter, on the other hand, would be a perfect item to store in Zone Two.

Your zones can be flexible as your business changes. If you find that you have items stored in Zone One that you rarely use, relocate them to either Zone Two or Zone Three, depending on their frequency of use. You might not even need to keep many of the items that you once

tip

Magazine boxes work well for storing many reference materials. Thin items that won't stand up by themselves in bookcases and don't have a spine wide enough to label can be grouped together by topic and stored in a magazine box. These include vendor catalogs, booklets for computer hardware, newsletters, and reports. Magazine boxes are available in wood, leather, plastic, and cardboard. One advantage of cardboard magazines boxes is that they can be trimmed if they're too tall to fit on your bookcase shelves.

thought were vitally important. Understand that you will always need to pay attention to what you have in your office at any given time so you can eliminate what is no longer giving you value. The more often you browse your paper and materials in the office, culling out the unnecessary, the easier it will be to maintain an organized space.

> **tip**
>
> Many people like to use three-ring binders for storing manuals, product literature, and other reference materials. If you have several binders you refer to regularly, be sure to label the spines in large, easily readable letters. This small, simple step will keep you from mistaking one binder for another and possibly taking the wrong one with you on a client call or to a meeting.

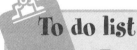

To do list

- ☐ Learn how to create a document retention policy
- ☐ Understand the benefits of a document retention policy

Reducing Paper Clutter: Creating a Document Retention Policy

As you learned previously in this chapter, paper is the biggest challenge when dealing with clutter in the workplace. Between printed emails, interoffice memos, invoices, purchase orders, client information, human resources files, financial paperwork, and business operations paperwork, it's easy to see how the paperless workplace is just a pipe dream. Often, employees will keep copies of paper in order to cover themselves just in case, or aren't sure what is important to keep versus what can be destroyed, and therefore end up keeping much more than necessary. This additional paper burden costs the company money in storage space as well as labor dollars to maintain the archives. One key step in reducing paper clutter is to create and maintain an effective document retention policy.

If you own your own small business, to save your company potential legal and administrative headaches down the road, it's important to establish a good *document retention policy (DRP)*, put it into writing, and consistently enforce it. A DRP is a policy that states what types of information get retained, for how long, and the date of destruction. The goal of a DRP is to be sure that the company retains everything required for as long as necessary and no longer.

Creating a policy whereby documents and information are systematically destroyed after a specified period of time will help keep your company archives from overflowing unnecessarily. A written document retention policy will also come in very handy and possibly be life-saving—at least from a legal standpoint—should your company ever find itself embroiled in a legal tangle and have its historic records subpoenaed.

As an employee, rather than a company-owner, following a document retention policy cuts down on your storage needs and can make essential documents easier to find. As mentioned earlier, find out whether your employer has a DRP, and then be sure to comply with it.

Summary

In this chapter you learned how to handle the influx of mail, bills, magazines, catalogs, and other business papers. We discussed the importance of processing mail and paper as often as possible to avoid getting caught up in a backlog and having to dig yourself out. You now understand how to appropriately store reference materials and how to create effective action files.

The F.A.I.T.H. model of paper management allows you to process paper through a system using five paths called File, Act, In Progress, Toss, and Hand Off. This system keeps paper moving so it doesn't get piled up and forgotten. We touched on the subject of using tickler files, how to create your own, and some of the different styles available. Finally, you learned the basics of creating a document retention policy and its benefits. In Chapter 9, "Organizing Your Computer," you'll learn how to organize your computer desktop, electronic documents, and email.

Organizing Your Computer

T he desktop computer is so widely used in workplaces around the world that it's hard to believe it's a relatively new invention. You'd be hard pressed to find a business person that doesn't have a desktop or laptop computer that she uses for work. Organizing your computer keeps your electronic data organized, saves you precious time, and helps you get the most value from your electronic system by conserving space on your hard drive. This chapter helps you get your computer and electronic files organized so you can easily and quickly find what you need when you need it. Information in this chapter applies to the Windows operating system, unless I have specifically indicated a Mac usage. The steps described in Windows may vary slightly, depending on your version of Windows.

In this chapter:

* Organizing your computer desktop
* Storing electronic documents
* Backing up data
* Managing email
* Using a contact manager and database
* Using a PDA

To do list

- [ ] Choose and apply desktop wallpaper
- [ ] Use shortcuts
- [ ] Organize desktop icons

Organizing Your Computer Desktop

Your computer might sit on your physical desktop, but your computer also has a desktop of its own. The screen that comes up after you turn your computer on and all your operating system and programs have loaded is called your *desktop*. Your desktop is comprised of two basic elements:

- Desktop *icons* represent programs, files, and folders of data stored within your computer
- Desktop *wallpaper* is simply the background image that appears on the desktop

You can control what your desktop looks like simply by changing the wallpaper image or how the icons are arranged.

Things You'll Need

- ❏   Computer and operating system software
- ❏   Electronic files for storage in your system

Choosing Wallpaper

The wallpaper is the image or pattern that serves as a background for your icons. Your computer could have something as simple as a solid color as the default wallpaper, or it might have your computer's logo or another image. Most people replace their default wallpaper with an image they like, such as a photo of friends, family, or a beautiful outdoor scene.

Replacing the wallpaper image is simple. If you use Windows, simply right-click anywhere on the desktop itself, and then click on Properties. You'll see a window that enables you to customize the image and other properties of your desktop. Just click on the Desktop, Background, or Wallpaper tab and you'll have the option to choose any of the built-in images. Alternatively, you can click the Browse button and choose your own image from anywhere on your hard drive.

If you use a Mac, go to your navigation bar, click on System Preferences, and under the tab called Personal, you'll see the Desktop and Screensaver button. From there, you can either choose one of the system's options or input your own image.

Creating and Using Shortcuts to Save Time

The icons on your desktop offer quick access to programs or documents without having to search for them through the computer's navigation bar, Windows Explorer, or Start menu. Shortcut icons are simply graphic images you can click to open the associated file or program. Shortcuts are visible on your desktop whenever you launch your operating system and are useful tools for quickly accessing documents or programs you use frequently.

Take time to put systems and routines in place to help streamline access to frequently used items or information. It costs you a bit of time up front, but it actually saves you time in the long run.

Creating shortcuts is a simple process. Let's say you use your Excel spreadsheet program every day and you want to put a shortcut for it on your desktop. First, go into the Start menu or navigation bar, choose Programs, and find the program named Excel. Right-click on the Excel listing, which opens a small menu. Drag your mouse to hover the cursor over the Send To option; in the menu that opens, choose Send to Desktop. The system automatically places a shortcut icon on your desktop. It's that easy. Now you can open Excel simply by double-clicking on the Excel shortcut icon on your desktop.

You can also create shortcuts to specific folders or documents you refer to often. For example, if you frequently need to access photographs or images for work that you have stored in your computer, you can create a shortcut to that actual folder on your desktop. Just go to My Computer or Windows Explorer and find the folder or document you want to put on the desktop. Right-click on the folder or document of your choice, point to the Send To option, and choose Send to Desktop. This action creates a new icon and shortcut on your desktop. When you want to access that folder or document, just double-click it from the desktop. Shortcuts are a terrific and simple way to give yourself fast access to the items you use frequently.

Organizing Your Icons

Desktop icons can really be a timesaver; however, if you're not careful, the desktop can be so covered with icons that it becomes a hindrance rather than a help for quickly finding and opening programs or document files. You can arrange your icons in several ways so they are a benefit and not a liability.

The first thing you can do to organize your icons is to delete any that are unused, old, or associated with programs you have uninstalled. Be sure that each icon is truly just a shortcut and not an actual document or application before deleting it. To check each icon, simply right-click

> **tip**
> Removing unnecessary icons from your desktop helps you clearly see what software you have on your computer. Decluttering the desktop also relieves the visual stress you experience from looking at so many icons all the time.

on it, choose Properties, and if the properties window says it's a shortcut, you have the option of deleting it without deleting any actual programs, documents, or folders. Another way to check if an icon is a shortcut is to look for a small arrow at the bottom-left corner of the icon. The arrow means it's a shortcut. If there is no arrow, it means the icon is an actual document, folder, or program.

After you've decluttered your desktop of unnecessary icons, you can choose to arrange your icons in logical groups or order. To arrange the icons automatically, right-click on any open space on the desktop and choose Arrange Icons. You have the option of choosing to arrange them by name, size, type, or date. If you want to arrange them manually, which is what many people choose, simply left-click on the icon and drag it to another spot on the desktop. If Windows won't let you manually move icons, you might have Auto Arrange selected. To disable Auto Arrange, just right-click on any open space on the desktop, point to Arrange Icons and then click on Auto Arrange, which will remove the selection. You should now be able to move your icons manually.

You can manually arrange icons any way you like, of course, but most people organize icons by frequency of use, by the type of program they represent, or just in a pattern that won't obscure the desktop image. For example, if you have a beautiful scenery image from your favorite vacation on your desktop, why cover it up with icons? Manually drag the icons to an area where they are out of the way and you can see the image.

On my desktop, I have a photo in the center that I love. Around the perimeter of my desktop, I've manually grouped icons in different rows according to their type of program. I have a row for creative programs (Word, Excel, Dreamweaver, and PowerPoint), a row for utilities (anti-virus, spyware checkers, and firewall), and a row for various folders such as My Photos, My Documents, and My Downloads. Grouping the shortcuts in this manner helps me quickly locate the one I want.

tip To arrange icons on a Mac, click on the desktop and click Finder Bar, View, Show View Options. At that point, you can choose icon size, text size, label position, and so forth. You have the option to arrange icons by name, date modified, date created, size, kind, or priority colored label.

To do list

- ❑ Learn to name electronic documents
- ❑ Effectively store electronic documents
- ❑ Create document templates

Storing Electronic Documents

Every time you create a new document, the first time you either close the document or click Save, you are asked what you'd like to name it and where you'd like to save it. Be sure you name documents using words that are relevant and indicate the content of the document. Also, it's important to understand where you're saving your documents. Many people get confused by the saving procedure, and by default, end up saving everything straight into the My Documents folder. This is the electronic equivalent of filing every paper you have in one big filing cabinet labeled Miscellaneous, with no rhyme or reason. This filing "system" does you no good because you very quickly discover that you have no way of finding anything you've saved. You then waste time (and electronic storage space) re-creating the same documents over again because you can't find the originals.

Things You'll Need

- ☐ Computer and operating system software
- ☐ Word processing program
- ☐ Electronic files for storage in your system

When saving documents, it's helpful to create subfolders beneath the main My Documents folder. Your subfolders should reflect the broad areas of your work and their titles should be easy to understand, such as Proposals, Clients, Forms, Personal, and so on. Organize the My Documents folder in such a way that very few items actually live in that direct folder; instead, they live in the appropriately named subfolders. The goal is to make it easy on yourself when searching for a document later.

Attention Speed Demons! I know it's tempting to save documents directly to the My Documents folder because it feels faster and you can just use the Find feature later when you need that document again. Don't fool yourself. Using the Find feature over and over again for the same documents is actually wasting more time than if you take a few moments to set up a subfolder system.

For keeping documents long-term versus short-term, some people find it helpful to temporarily store active or in-process documents in an Active Projects folder on the desktop. This folder should be viewed as simply a temporary holding pen for things you're working on and not a permanent home for anything. The desktop icon gives you quick access to these projects while you're working on them. After you're finished with a project, give it a permanent home inside a subfolder in My Documents or another appropriate place.

Examples of what to keep in a temporary Active Projects folder would be a writing project, a half-finished business letter, or anything else you're working on and still making changes to.

> **tip**
> If you choose to make an Active Projects folder for your desktop, be sure to open it at the end of each week to review what is there so you don't accidentally leave something there long-term.

CREATING TEMPLATES

To avoid re-creating the same document over and over again, create a template to save you a ton of time and energy. A *template* is a document guide that automatically sets up the formatting—margins, font size, line spacing—and even text content of a new document. Templates are useful for business letters, invoices, memos, newsletters, and other types of documents that you create frequently. Templates are simple to create in Word. First, create the document you want to make into a template for future use. Then go to the File menu and choose Save As a Document Template. Type a name into the File Name box for your template and click OK. Unless you specify otherwise, templates are saved to the default Templates folder. When you need to use that same document again, just go to your Templates folder (under My Documents), open it up, and choose the template. Keep in mind that versions of Word differ from each other, so your version might not show the Templates folder in the My Documents folder. It might be located in another spot on your C: drive. Just go to the Start menu, point to Find files or folders and type in *template*. After you find the location of the folder, make a shortcut for it on your desktop and you'll always be able to access it.

You can also create a new template by modifying an existing, preloaded template. Click File, New, and from the dialog box that pops up, choose a template that is similar to the one you want to create. Choose the Template radio button at the bottom of the dialog box and then create your template. When you're finished, close the document and you're done. Creating templates is one way to save time and energy as well as to ensure that the documents you create are all consistent.

To do list

- ☐ Learn options for backing up important data
- ☐ Choose a backup plan and schedule

Backing Up Your Data

You wouldn't jump out of an airplane without a backup parachute, would you? Heck, you might not jump out of an airplane at all, but anyone who has gone sky-diving will tell you that you *always* have a backup chute ready in case your primary chute malfunctions. Every day, you conduct important business on your computer, you make documents, you might use financial software, and all these things are important. But I'm willing to bet that you don't have a backup schedule in place.

Things You'll Need

- ☐ Data to back up
- ☐ Backup media

If you do regular data backups, that is terrific! If you don't back your data up, however, you're treading dangerous waters. It isn't a question of if your hard drive will fail, but *when*. Backing up your data is a task you should be scheduling regularly, no less than weekly, and some experts recommend you conduct backups daily. It used to be that you could back up data from software and your documents onto floppy disks, but not anymore. Most computers don't come with floppy drives and many files are too large to fit on a floppy disk anyway, so you'll need to back up your data in a different way.

There are two kinds of computer files:

- *Data* that you generate and create yourself, such as correspondence, forms, accounting records, contact names, spreadsheets, graphic images, and so on
- *Programs*, such as Word, Excel, PageMaker, and so on

There is no need to back up the actual programs unless you've lost the original CDs that came with the software. Using these CDs, the programs can easily be re-installed. After the programs are re-installed, they will need to be repopulated with your old data backups. If you do ever re-install a program from a CD, remember to go online to check for security updates and patches so your program is up-to-date.

Backup Options

There are many types of media you can use for backing up your files, including floppy disks, tapes, removable hard drives, Zip drives, flash drives, rewritable CD-ROMs, and portable USB hard drives. It's preferable to back up to a media type you understand and find simple to use. After all, the simpler you make it, the more likely you are to do it. It's also a good idea to choose a media type that can accommodate enough data so you can put a copy of all your information in one place. If you have questions about the various kinds of backup media, consult a computer specialist who can explain the pros, cons, and costs of each one and can recommend one based on your specific needs.

For additional security, consider having two physical backups. Do a daily backup that you keep in the office in the event that your computer gets stolen or the hard drive crashes. Do a weekly or monthly backup that you keep off-site in case of a natural disaster. This will involve trading backups each week or month to be sure that the one off-site is the most recent.

There are also secure online backup services you can subscribe to if you prefer to avoid doing backups yourself. Subscriptions to services such as Streamload (www.streamload. com) offer free data backup for anything up to 10GB of data. After you exceed 10GB, prices range from as little as $4.95 a month up to $40 a month, depending on how much data you want to store. Another online backup subscription service is EVault (www.evault.com) that offers plans for small, medium, and large businesses.

tip

When backing up data, keep a second copy of your backup in another location for safety reasons. If your building should burn or a natural disaster occur, it could destroy the backup you keep in the office. Having an additional backup off-site spreads out your risk and increases the likelihood that you'll be able to recover your data. You don't want to lose both the original and the copy.

Choosing Your Backup Plan

Whatever you decide to do in terms of backup media and frequency, the whole point of backing up data is to minimize and avoid risk. You get to choose the level of risk with which you're most comfortable. When you back up daily, you only risk losing a day's worth of information. If you choose to back up every week, you risk losing a week's worth of information. When you are planning your backup strategy, think long and hard about just how much you are willing to risk your company data and create your schedule accordingly.

Here are the types of data you should include in your backups:

- Web pages you've created
- Photos and other images
- Documents you've created
- Important correspondence
- Financial/accounting data
- Internal documents, such as memos
- Databases
- Contact management information
- Calendars
- Email
- Bookmarks in your browser

To do list

❏ Use electronic folders to sort email
❏ Block and delete spam

Managing Email

The advent of email has completely changed the way business is conducted. Email has become our new master and because it's instant communication, we are no longer content to wait for phone calls, faxes, or letters. We want a response and we want it *now*! The ease of email is also its greatest drawback; it's easy to send way too much email with just the click of a button. Not only can you accidentally send messages to the wrong recipients, but you can be quickly buried in email in a very short time.

The email *inbox* is a place created for email to land and wait to be read, just like your physical mailbox at your home. You don't go to your mailbox, take out what you want to read, and leave the rest there for tomorrow, do you? I bet you do that with your email inbox, though. The inbox should just be a place where unread mail lives until you read it, delete it, act on it, or file it away. Email is much like paper in that if it stagnates in the inbox, it piles up and causes disorganization and confusion.

Set up folders in your email program so that after you're finished reading an email, you can move it to a folder and save it (only *if* it's worth keeping for future reference). Your folders will change over time, and you can add and delete them as you discover what kind of email you tend to keep. Setting up folders for clients, friends, family, projects, and anything else that you feel is relevant in your life will keep you organized, and you'll know where to find a message if you need it.

The email messages you save in your inbox, outbox, and folders are an electronic history of your correspondence with many people. These documents contain a tremendous amount of information that can be helpful in the future, assuming you know how to find the specific email you need. If you know an old email contains information you need, you can find the email any number of ways.

You can sort email by date, sender's name, or subject. In most email programs, you can sort by opening a folder and clicking on the column heading you want to use as your primary sorting field. In addition, most email programs offer a handy Find feature. This feature enables you to search emails by entering search terms, which the program looks for in any part of any email.

Creating file folders for saving email requires the ability to make decisions about the email in the moment that you're reading it. Either delete it or move it to a folder to save it. Putting off decision-making about your email only delays the decision and action. You'll need to do it someday, so you might as well get it done today. Otherwise, you'll end up taking an entire day down the road to sit and review a thousand old emails you didn't want to deal with right away. The old saying goes, "You can pay me now or you can pay me later," right? It surely applies in this case because email piles up very quickly. It's important that you can keep up with it so you don't find yourself drowning in it.

SAY NO TO SPAM

Part of the reason email is such a problem is the presence of spam. *Spam* is just a word that means unsolicited or junk email. I receive approximately 100 or more spam messages a day that I simply delete. To help block spam, you can enable filters within your email client, if they are available. Outlook 2003 has easily configured junk filters. They identify what they think is spam and filter it into a Junk folder for your review and deletion. Eudora has the same filters if you choose to use them. They are easy to set up, but do be careful, as not everything that ends up in the spam folder is actually spam. Filters have been known to catch a few legitimate emails, so give the Junk folder a quick review before deleting it all in one fell swoop.

Your Internet service provider (ISP) might also offer you spam blocking capability at the server level. Go to its website and do a search for the word *spam* to see what it offers. It should be free and easy to set up. You can also purchase third-party spam blockers, such as Norton AntiSpam, Mailwasher, and McAfee SpamKiller, among many others. You just pay online and download the latest versions, configure them to filter your email, and you're all set. If your budget is stretched thin, many free spam-blocking programs are available online for downloading if you search for the term *spam blocker* in your favorite search engine.

Using Contact Management Software

In today's busy business climate, things move really fast. It's tough to stay caught up, organized, and on top of things without relying on some type of contact management software. Contact management software makes it simple to keep up with the progress and past history of any one of your business contacts. Each contact has its own record in which you can keep the address, phone numbers, business title, notes, and countless other pieces of information pertaining to that person or business.

The only way to enter information into a contact manager is by first setting up a basic contact file for the information to be attached to. After you set up the contact file by adding a name, address, and telephone number, you can then attach any number of tasks to that contact. You can schedule appointments, phone calls, and emails; make notes; track sales history; and create a group for that specific type of contact.

One of the tools available to busy professionals is a handheld personal digital assistant (PDA). These are manufactured by a number of companies, including Dell, palmOne (formerly Palm), Hewlett-Packard, and many others. Handheld devices are small enough that they can be carried in a briefcase, purse, or suit pocket, but powerful enough to keep your entire calendar and contact information right at your fingertips. PDAs offer more functionality today than ever before; some units come with wireless connectivity to the Internet and also double as a mobile phone. It's the best of all worlds!

PDAs are a great way to be prepared to schedule a meeting, make a call, send a letter, or just jot a few important notes when you are away from your computer. They are also a terrific alternative to a paper planner because you can use them to add new contacts directly into your contact manager, schedule recurring events, quickly reschedule appointments without erasing, store color images, and in many cases, create and edit documents.

Your PDA, whichever one you choose to purchase, will synchronize data with your contact manager, such as ACT!, Outlook, or Lotus Notes. The sync function is usually done via a cable and only takes a few seconds. It's important to sync your PDA with your computer daily so both calendars are up-to-date at all times. When you sync regularly, you also have a backup of your data on your computer in case your PDA get lost or stolen.

Summary

This chapter helped you organize your computer, from the desktop to the documents. You learned how to create and organize your shortcuts and how to store your electronic information so you can find it again. PDAs, contact management software, and removable data storage and backup are all important parts of getting your computer organized, too. Your computer is arguably the most important business tool you own, so keeping it organized will help you be successful and reach your business goals.

Chapter 10, "Staying Organized on the Road," discusses how to stay organized when you travel. If you work from your car or fly from city to city for work, you'll find tips and ideas to make the most of being on the road.

Staying Organized on the Road

I n recent years, video conferencing and tele-conferencing have made it possible for business people to travel less often, which adds up to significant time and money savings. Face-to-face meetings are still a necessity for a tremendous number of business people, however, and for some, being on the road is a way of life. If you travel for business, whether by car or plane, this chapter will help you stay organized, be productive, and make the most of your travel time. You learn how to keep all of your traveling office components—computer, paperwork, briefcase, and so on—organized and fully functional. You also learn how to make the most of your time on the road (and in the hotel).

To do list

- ☐ Choose the right briefcase for you
- ☐ Organize your briefcase for travel
- ☐ Learn to prepare for a business trip
- ☐ Create a travel checklist

Choosing and Organizing Your Briefcase

Your briefcase is an important business tool. It's your mobile office, holding all the other items that keep you functioning and productive away from the office. To serve you most effectively, your briefcase should be functional, easy to transport, and have ample room for all the essential business tools you take on the road with you. Your briefcase should also look attractive and professional and reflect your personal style.

The first step to organizing your briefcase is to be sure you use a briefcase that is right for you. We've all made buying mistakes and if you bought a briefcase that just isn't working for you, that's okay. I've done it myself. If the one you purchased isn't quite what you need, donate or sell it and buy a different one more suited to your needs. A few basic features to look for when choosing a briefcase are

- A removable shoulder strap for when you travel
- Interior compartments to help organize various items
- A reliable closing mechanism to keep information safe
- An attractive and professional appearance
- Durable materials and construction

Organizing Your Briefcase Contents

You can keep your briefcase organized by always keeping items in the same spot inside the case. This habit enables you to be able to locate an item quickly rather than having to dig through papers and other supplies to find it. It also makes you look professional to others when you open your briefcase and it's neat and organized.

Compartmentalizing is the name of the game when using a briefcase. The natural movement of your walking shifts small items and loose papers, causing them to intermingle and making everything hard to find again. If the briefcase you choose has two large main sections, consider designating each section for a different purpose. Perhaps use one of the sections for information relating to clients, and the other one for supplies and personal reading material. Or you could designate one section for items to be worked on, and the other side for items you've finished. A third option is to use one section for information relating to people you've already seen on your trip and the other for people you're still waiting to see.

If your case has one large section with a number of small pockets and compartments, use

> **tip** You can increase the number of separate compartments simply by adding small zipper pouches, hinged boxes, or other small portable containers inside your briefcase. Use these small tools to keep pens, office supplies, medication, tissues, receipts, coins and dollar bills for tipping, or anything else that might migrate here and there inside your briefcase.

the provided compartments and then subdivide the large section even more by adding extra organizing tools. File folders, pocket folders, and closed-end file jackets are great for keeping information separate and easy to find inside the briefcase.

As you would with any container, be sure to designate a specific use for each one and use them consistently so you don't end up with several pouches randomly filled with unrelated items. The whole point of using the extra compartments is to make it *easier* to find things, not to search through every container looking for one item because you never put it the same place twice.

Clutter is a collection of unrelated objects living together. Containers that have no specific purpose will always collect clutter—even in your briefcase. Label and designate containers for specific uses whenever possible.

Choosing the Things You'll Carry

What you carry with you in your briefcase is your choice, but before you try to pack everything but the kitchen sink, really think about what you use every day and how important each item is. If you're willing to risk it, try carrying fewer items and take the attitude that if you absolutely do need something you didn't bring, you can buy or rent it when you get to your destination. Careful evaluation of each item will ensure that you don't over-pack your briefcase.

Make it a habit to empty out and reorganize your briefcase weekly. Establishing good maintenance habits keeps your briefcase functional and prevents you from building up several weeks' worth of clutter and paper. Keeping your briefcase clean and organized boosts your self-confidence and projects a professional image to your colleagues, clients, and prospects.

> **note** Suggested items to pack in your briefcase:
> - Pad of paper/portfolio
> - Pens/pencils/highlighter
> - PDA with charger cord
> - Reading material
> - Client or business files
> - Wrapped snack
> - Breath mints or spray
> - Important travel documents
> - Small travel umbrella
> - Your business cards
> - An extra pair of hosiery (for ladies)
> - An extra tie (for men)

PREPARING FOR YOUR BUSINESS TRIP

Setting up consistent pretravel routines makes your leaving easier and smoother, especially if you travel regularly. Here are some tips:

＊ Keep a travel case of toiletries packed and ready to go at all times. Switching bottles back and forth from your home to your suitcase increases the risk of losing or forgetting important items.

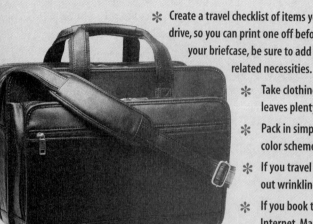

✳ Create a travel checklist of items you need on every trip and keep it on your computer hard drive, so you can print one off before each trip. In addition to the things you normally carry in your briefcase, be sure to add client files, medication, your plane ticket, and other travel-related necessities.

✳ Take clothing to the cleaners the week before you leave, if possible. This leaves plenty of time for you to pick it up.

✳ Pack in simple color schemes so all your clothing can mix and match. One color scheme also enables you to pack fewer accessories.

✳ If you travel frequently, buy specific clothing pieces that travel well without wrinkling and build your travel wardrobe around them.

✳ If you book travel online, check in from home or the office using the Internet. Many airlines will also allow you to print out your boarding pass in advance. These steps are tremendous time-savers because you avoid waiting in unnecessary airport lines.

✳ Wear your bulkiest shoes and suit to save space in your luggage so you can avoid checking any bags. Waiting in lines to check your bags through and claiming bags at the other end eats up a lot of time.

✳ Call ahead to the hotel you're staying in and ask if it provides items such as shampoo, conditioner, soap, hair dryers, and irons. Making sure you can get these items at the hotel means you can leave those items at home, saving space in your luggage.

To do list

☐ Learn about laptop carrying options
☐ Choose the right laptop case
☐ Protect your laptop and data when traveling

Traveling with Your Computer

More and more people are relying solely on laptops rather than having a desktop computer and a laptop. This change streamlines office space, but it also means that it's more important than ever to safeguard your laptop when you travel. Laptops are a popular item for thieves to target because of their high dollar value and small size. Taking care to keep your laptop safe is an investment in your peace of mind, as well as in the safety of your confidential business, personal, and financial information.

Things You'll Need

- ❏ Laptop computer
- ❏ Laptop case or bag

Laptop Cases and Sleeves

The first thing to consider when traveling with your laptop is how you'll be carrying it. You can purchase a laptop case or you can use a laptop sleeve in conjunction with a standard travel bag. The sheer volume of laptop-carrying options is staggering. With so many options, you can choose the one that is just perfect for your needs. You can spend as little as $29 or as much as several hundred dollars, depending on the quality and features you want.

A laptop *case* is a bag dedicated to the purpose of carrying and protecting your laptop. It can be soft or hard-sided. It might have additional compartments for carrying cords, discs, and other supplies, but its main function is to carry and protect a laptop computer. In the past, this kind of bag has been bulky and largely unattractive. Today, manufacturers are creating stylish laptop cases that not only look good but protect well, too.

A laptop *sleeve* is a padded fabric or hard-shell "envelope" that you place your laptop inside, and then you carry the entire sleeve inside another bag. Laptop sleeves are good for camouflaging your laptop to reduce the likelihood of theft. Laptop sleeves are also handy for consolidating baggage—especially for women, who often travel with a briefcase, a purse, *and* a carry-on bag. A protective sleeve enables you to slip the laptop right into a briefcase or carry-on bag.

Here are a few of the available features that laptop cases offer:

- Durable outer fabric or hard shell case
- Versatile carrying strap configuration
- Lightweight for easy carrying
- Compartments for cords, discs, and supplies
- Plenty of padding for impact and shock absorption
- Wheels for easy transport and reducing back strain
- Stylish appearance

When choosing a laptop case, you probably won't find one with all of the listed features. Remember to focus on choosing a laptop case with the features *you* need and that will make *you* feel most comfortable when traveling.

The BackOffice Case

Shaun Jackson Design has come up with what I consider to be the most innovative laptop case yet, called The BackOffice. It's called The BackOffice because it's like an office you can carry on your back. It can be used as a backpack, it has a shoulder strap for carrying vertically and a removable sleeve, and it opens up into a flat workstation.

The BackOffice is lightweight and looks attractive when closed up. When you need to work, it literally unfolds in seconds into a flat laptop workstation, complete with pockets for keeping peripherals and office supplies at your fingertips. The BackOffice is soft-sided, made of black ballistics nylon, and has a nonslip surface for working on your lap, an airplane tray, or in a train or car. The sturdy flat workstation spans your entire lap, eliminating the hassle of trying to balance your computer across your legs while you type.

The BackOffice was designed with enough storage space to house your laptop, supplies, cables, cords, papers, and files. The multifunctional BackOffice combines the features of a briefcase, backpack and laptop bag, streamlining travel by replacing your briefcase (see Figure 10.1).

FIGURE 10.1
The BackOffice bag looks like a regular laptop bag when closed, but it becomes a sturdy workstation when opened. (Photos used with permission.)

You can also remove the computer sleeve from The BackOffice when you wish to travel even lighter. It fits well inside other luggage and still offers padded protection for your laptop. The separate sleeve is another example of the versatility of The BackOffice.

The BackOffice bags come in two sizes. If you have a 15" or smaller computer, you can use

tip
Shaun Jackson Design has also incorporated another innovation into its products called the Cooldeck. The Cooldeck system keeps the laptop raised above the surface of The BackOffice. This buffer space lets air circulate underneath the computer, keeping both the machine and your legs cooler.

the standard The BackOffice. If your computer is larger than 15", you'll need The Big BackOffice that accommodates screens up to 17" across. The standard The BackOffice retails for $149.95, while The Big BackOffice retails at $179.95. You can purchase these and other quality bags directly from the Shaun Jackson Design website at www.sjdesign.com.

The Brain Cell Laptop Case

Another innovative designer of laptop bags and cases is Tom Bihn. This company designs a number of bags for varying uses, but in this section, we'll talk about one of its laptop bags, called the Brain Cell, shown in Figure 10.2. The Brain Cell is a hard-sided case made of corrugated plastic and covered in Cordura nylon. It can be carried stylishly on its own or used as a laptop sleeve by slipping it inside of another bag or suitcase. The hard sides of the Brain Cell offer protection from crushing and the laptop sits in a specially constructed compartment inside the bag. The Brain Cell uses this unique system to help protect your laptop if it is dropped.

The case itself weighs in at right around one pound. The Brain Cell closes on the top, and is held closed with two padded Velcro strips. The Brain Cell is available in five colors and has an exterior elastic mesh pocket on the front for carrying papers, files, additional media, cables, or peripherals.

FIGURE 10.2
The Brain Cell is a streamlined, versatile bag that can stand alone or fit easily inside other bags or luggage. (Photo used with permission.)

The Brain Cell is available in six sizes and is quite affordable, at just $50. You can purchase these and other quality bags on the Tom Bihn website at www.tombihn.com.

Protecting Your Laptop and Its Data

A client I'll call Bob (not his real name) was traveling out of town on business to assist in a court case for one of his clients. Part of his job was to use his laptop to run a PowerPoint presentation for those in the courtroom. During the course of the morning, Bob ran the presentation for the judge and jury, the witnesses were examined, and testimony was given. At noon, the judge called for a lunch break. Assuming a court of law to be a safe environment, everyone left for lunch, leaving several laptop computers in the room unattended. Upon returning from lunch an hour later, Bob discovered his laptop had been stolen, along with everyone else's. This experience illustrates that you can never assume your laptop is safe from theft. You must be extra aware when traveling with your laptop. Computer theft is a real concern, and you can lessen your risk with a bit of common sense. Safety tips for laptop travel include

- Camouflage your laptop by protecting it with a laptop sleeve and carrying it inside a regular piece of luggage. You can also camouflage your laptop by purchasing a laptop case that is designed to *not* look like a computer bag.

- Never leave your laptop unattended, even for a second, in the airport or on a bus or train.

- If you must doze in an airport, wrap the strap of your laptop bag strap around your ankle or wrist and keep the bag next to your body.

- When traveling on a train that has a special area for luggage, keep your laptop with you in your seat. Thieves know to look for computer bags in the luggage area and they can be off the train with your laptop before you can even get up out of your seat.

- Invest in a laptop locking cable for those times when you absolutely must leave your laptop in your hotel room.

To do list

❏ Learn about travel file organizers
❏ Choose the right organizer for your travel needs

Traveling with Paperwork: Filing Organizers

Taking time to keep paper files and information organized when traveling will make your return home easier, whether you're returning from a day on the road or three days in another city. You can get back to the office and right to work rather than spending time wrapping up loose ends from your trip.

If you travel in your car most of the time, you probably need to carry a good bit of paperwork and files with you on the road. Several good products are on the market for storing and retrieving paper files in the car. The travel file box is one of the most popular items for keeping files in the car and we talked about it in Chapter 6, "Choosing Filing Storage and Supplies." The travel file box has a hinged lid that latches closed and a carrying handle. Many companies manufacture this kind of product and it's a great option for those who work from their cars or have to transport files from their office to home and back again.

Smead also makes a good tool for travel filing, called the Smead Inndura Ultracolor Transport Files, shown in Figure 10.3. These inexpensive, expanding file boxes are handy for keeping files organized in the car. You can purchase the Inndura Ultracolor for around $12. They are portable, lightweight, made of flexible plastic, and have separate compartments with top tabs for filing information easily. A large plastic flap keeps them closed and because they're plastic, they keep your papers inside dry and protected from the weather when you are taking them to and from the car.

FIGURE 10.3
Expanding plastic files keep papers separate and easy to access. (Photo used with permission.)

Another version of the expanding file is the CitySmart Expanding File from Pendaflex (see Figure 10.4). These file holders have either 7 or 13 interior sections for keeping papers separate and use Velcro closures to keep files secure. The two-tone look is stylish and professional and they are available in three colors. Pick up the CitySmart Expanding File at any office supply store for $11.

Another organizing tool to store and file papers while you're on the road is the Smead Inndura Carry File, shown in Figure 10.5. This is a unique organizing tool because not only can it keep your papers separated in individual sleeves like the expanding file does, it is sturdier and more professional looking than a standard expanding file. The Inndura Carry File is hard-sided and resembles a briefcase. It has a hard plastic handle on top and a front closure to keep files covered and intact. It is also waterproof and has 12 pockets for storing information.

Making Use of Travel Downtime

When traveling by plane, you'll have a significant amount of downtime that you can fritter away reading a novel or you can choose to use more productively. Not that there is anything wrong with reading a novel—in fact, sometimes waiting in the airport is the only time some people have to relax and do some personal reading. Balance is a good thing in your life.

Things You'll Need

❑ Business cards
❑ Contact manager or planner
❑ Reading material
❑ Memo recorder, writing material, or laptop computer
❑ Credit card statements, checkbook

If you prefer to take advantage of downtime to get work done, that's okay, too. Waiting in lines, waiting at the gate to take off, and actual flying time are good times to catch up on things that it's difficult to make time for at the office, such as paperwork, reports, or reviewing a presentation. Also, travel time is a good time to take care of personal tasks that you might not make time for at home. Get a haircut, manicure, or pedicure; do some shopping; have a massage; get your shoes shined; write and address birthday cards for the month; or even just relax and meditate.

Here are just a few business-oriented tasks you can do during travel downtime:

- Go through and organize business cards, tossing out those that are no longer valuable or relevant.
- Add new contacts to your database.
- Prepare expense reports.
- Listen to books on CD.
- Make phone calls that will strengthen your business relationships with clients, prospects, or vendors.
- Handwrite follow-up notes and thank-you notes to clients, prospects, and vendors.
- Catch up on business reading of articles, reports, or white papers.
- Catch up on business writing. Compose letters, articles, memos, and presentations during wait times.
- Review your credit card statements or balance your checkbook.

To do list

❑ Get the most from hotel concierge services
❑ Assess hotel business services
❑ Choose the right hotel for your needs

Making the Most of Your Hotel Stay

Business travel almost always requires a stay in a hotel of some sort. Unless you travel by car in a specific territory, you'll rarely encounter a business trip that begins and ends the same day. Whether you stay in a budget motel or five-star accommodations, there are ways to make your hotel stay more enjoyable and productive. The hotel's concierge and business services can offer assistance that can make your stay easier and more productive.

tip
The longer your stay, the more important your comfort and amenities are, so factor that into your decision as well. A budget hotel might be perfectly fine for a quick overnight trip, but if you're out of town for a conference or a week of sales meetings, a hotel with more amenities will be a better choice for both comfort and convenience.

FINDING THE RIGHT BUSINESS AMENITIES

Many hotels cater to business travelers, offering several amenities that were unheard of in years past. You're unlikely to find a hotel that offers all of these amenities, but look for one that includes those that are most important to you:

* An onsite business center for faxing and copies
* Free local phone calls
* Free high-speed Internet connections in the room
* Dry cleaning, pressing/laundry service
* Express check-out
* Hairdryers and irons in the room
* Safes to lock your valuables and laptops
* Free shuttle to and from the airport
* Free continental breakfast
* Nonsmoking rooms
* Mail center with overnight package shipping
* Free swimming pool, spa, or fitness center
* Free shoeshine services
* Complementary daily newspaper

Using the Hotel Concierge

The term *concierge* is a French word that describes a hotel staff member who attends to guests' needs by handling tasks such as luggage storage, taking and delivering messages, and making reservations for tours, just to name a few. In recent years, many hotels have gone above and beyond in offering extended concierge services for guests.

The hotel concierge is happy to take care of things you might not have time to do yourself, such as having your suit pressed and delivered to your room the night before your big meeting or helping you locate replacements for lost or forgotten toiletry items. If the concierge really can't take care of something you need, he or she will do everything possible to figure out who can. The nice thing is that hotels don't charge for their concierge service. You should, of course, expect to incur charges for the products or services they arrange for you, such as dinner reservations, event tickets, or a cocktail party for your clients.

note Some hotels offer what is called the *concierge floor*. Although the rooms are more expensive, concierge floor guests receive additional services and amenities, such as complementary breakfast, lunch and snack buffets, complementary cocktails, and check-out times as late as 6 p.m. The more upscale the hotel, the more you can expect in concierge service. The Ritz Carlton, for example, offers a technology butler at many of its locations. This onsite information technology expert is available 24/7 to troubleshoot guests' technology challenges.

Using the Hotel Business Center

Most hotels offer some kind of onsite business center for guest use. When you make your reservation, ask what equipment is available for guest use in the business center and what the hours of operation are. Some are open 24/7 and accessible with a guest room key, while others have set hours of business.

Items you're likely to find in a business center include

- Fax machine
- Internet-ready computer(s)
- Printer
- Data port for your laptop
- Black-and-white copier
- Color copier
- Paper cutter
- Scissors, paper clips, and stapler

Be sure you find out in advance what are the charges, if any, for using the business center. More and more hotels are offering this amenity free of charge, but there are still hotels that charge per minute for Internet service, plus per page for faxing and making copies. As long as you know up front what to expect, you won't be surprised when you get the bill.

Summary

In this chapter you got ideas to help you stay organized when you travel for business, whether it's by plane or car. You learned about organizing your briefcase as well as various laptop storage options, and how to carry files on the road. Making good use of downtime when you travel is another great way to be productive, even when you're away from home, and you now know how to use your hotel stay to your best advantage from beginning to end. Traveling can be stressful but this chapter gave you a lot of good tips for making it simpler and more enjoyable.

Chapter 11, "Using Vertical Space to Organize," gives you ideas and product information about how to use the available vertical space in your office or home office. Vertical spaces such as walls, doors, and the sides of furniture can be used for storage and organization, which helps you find what you need when you need it.

Part IV

Simple Storage Solutions

Using Vertical Space to Organize

In this chapter:

* Learn to spot unused storage space
* Use the vertical space in your office
* Learn about best organizational tools

Look around your home or office and try to identify additional storage space. Are you thinking of how you can add more furniture to increase the flat surfaces, drawers, and cabinets? We're so accustomed to relying on furnishings for storage that we often forget we can actually create storage where none exists. To do that, we simply need to take a close look at unused space in our offices and think of creative ways to use it.

To understand the possibilities of small spaces, consider the way offices occupy space within a large city, where real estate is at a premium. Because small lots don't accommodate the sprawling offices of the suburbs, urban architects build *up*, rather than out. By taking advantage of vertical and other unused spaces in your office, you can create valuable new storage areas without expanding your office area. It takes a little creativity to take advantage of all available space, however. This chapter teaches you how to be aware of hidden and creative storage areas that you might not have thought of before, and it describes ideas and tools you can use to make the most of whatever space you have.

To do list

❑ Calculate the cubic feet within your office space
❑ Locate unused spaces you can convert to storage and measure them

Sizing Up Your Free Space

The first step to using your space to its fullest potential is to make sure you begin noticing the space in the first place. You can't use something you're not aware of, after all. You need to begin thinking like a designer and envision your space not in flat square feet, but in cubic feet—in 3-D if you will—and no glasses required!

Things You'll Need

❑ Calculator
❑ Measuring tape
❑ Pencil/paper

Thinking in Terms of Cubic Feet

A room has length and width (the obvious dimensions), but don't forget height. If you have an office that's 10' by 10', you have 100 square feet of floor space. However, if you have 8-foot ceilings, you actually have *800 cubic feet* to work with. Granted, you can't realistically fill every inch from floor to ceiling with boxes and furniture, but learning to think in terms of cubic feet helps you notice potential storage areas you've overlooked. Some areas to consider include

tip
To calculate cubic feet of any space, simply multiply the length by the width by the height of a space. For example, if your space is 8' by 10' with 8-foot ceilings, your equation looks like this:
Length × Width × Height
$8 \times 10 \times 8 = 640$ cubic feet

- **Above doorways**—Single narrow shelves fit above door openings for storing infrequently accessed items such as computer manuals and software boxes.
- **The backs of closet doors**—Hooks on the backs of closet doors hold jackets, backpacks, or laptop cases. Over-door racks can be used for storing media such as VHS tapes, CDs, and DVDs.

- **The sides of furniture or file cabinets**—Create homes for papers by attaching bins, hooks, or cork board to the sides of file cabinets, desks, or bookcases.
- **The walls**—Storage shelves can be wall-mounted for storing books, office supplies, computer peripherals, and much more.

Working with Vertical Space

After you notice the available vertical space in your office that you want to make use of, measure it and roughly sketch it out on paper. Draw in rough representations of windows and furniture surrounding the space. After you have it measured and drawn, you'll be able to begin thinking about which organizing and storage tools would work best for you in those spaces.

When measuring confined wall space—wall space with hard boundaries on either side, such as another wall or a window—take your horizontal measurements at two or three different points. Walls and windows are rarely built perfectly square in any building, and even though it might look fine to the naked eye, even a half inch of difference from top to bottom could cause problems during installation of shelving.

Always measure in at least two spots, preferably three, and use the smallest of the measurements as your guide, as shown in Figure 11.1.

FIGURE 11.1
Even a small difference between the top and bottom measurements of a confined space can cause problems when you begin installing shelving.

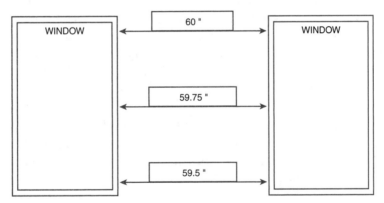

To do list

- ☐ Consider the use of free-standing or wall-mounted bookshelves in your office
- ☐ Learn to install wall-mounted and floating shelves
- ☐ Use storage cubes, wall-bins, and racks

Choosing and Using Tools for Vertical Storage

There are many organizing and storage tools to choose from when making use of your vertical space. You can use shelves of all kinds, free-standing racks, and stacking storage cubes. The tools you choose all depend on the size of the space and the purpose you want it to serve. If you need extra space for keeping papers, notebooks, or folders, you need a different tool than if you want to store books or software. Before you choose a tool, think through the size and shape of the item you want to store and make sure that the tool and the item work together. For example, if you're making room to store small boxes of various office supplies, choose a container or storage tool that will hold an adequate number of boxes while keeping them visible and easily accessible. The perfect tool might be a set of crystal-clear acrylic stacking drawers you can set on a shelf. The square sides of the drawers work well with the square sides of each box of supplies and the sliding action of the drawers makes the contents easy to access when you need them.

It's important that you use storage tools wisely to get the most from the space they offer. I once worked with a client who had a beautiful executive office with handsome built-in bookshelves. She had a few books scattered about on the shelves, but the majority of the space was taken up with stacked client files, office supplies, software CDs, and piles of loose paper. Her desk was cluttered with personal items such as framed photos, awards, and a few small sculptures from her travels. While the bookshelves were full of everything *but* books, there were stacks of books on the floor under her desk. This was a simple case of using the wrong tool for the wrong job. We began by clearing everything off the bookshelves, sorting the items into categories, and then pulling the books out from under the desk and removing all her personal items from her desktop. After we had sorted these items into categories, we began relocating each category into a more appropriate place.

We created homes for the loose papers by using inexpensive magnetic bins on the side of a steel file cabinet, and I gave her a step file sorter for keeping active files on her desktop (learn more about these tools in Chapter 6, "Choosing Filing Storage and Supplies"). Office supplies and software CDs were relocated into the closet because they didn't require everyday access. Finally, we loaded all the books onto the bookshelves, leaving space between groupings of books for all her special personal items that had been cluttering her desk. All this work only took a few hours and in the end she had an office that made her feel like the successful businesswoman she was.

Using Bookshelves to Add Storage

Bookshelves can be permanently built into a room or they can be free-standing and moveable. Bookshelves are great for books (obviously), but not so great for much else. Because they are designed for a specific purpose, it's best to use them for that purpose and find alternative storage for loose papers, files, and other office items.

Even though bookshelves are best for storing books, if space is truly scarce in your office and you don't have enough books to fill your shelves, you *can* adapt bookshelves to store other items effectively. You can store magazines and many other items on bookshelves by adding open baskets, boxes, stacking trays, hanging file boxes, or magazine files.

When buying bookshelves, you'll have more flexibility and storage options if you get adjustable shelves. Fixed shelves might look a little bit nicer but most people appreciate having the option to move each individual shelf as their storage needs change. If you'll be storing a lot of heavy books, spread them out over the entire bookshelf to distribute their weight, rather than keeping them all on one shelf. Putting too many heavy books on one shelf might make the shelf sag in the center over time. Another option if you have heavy books is to purchase two shorter sets of bookshelves rather than one long shelf. The longer the shelf supporting the books, the more likely it is to sag. A shorter shelf resists sagging in the center under the weight of heavy books.

> **tip**
> It's fine to use bookshelves for your personal items, such as trophies, framed photos, and art pieces, but not if it means storing some of your books on the floor. Books have first priority and decorative items get sprinkled in after all the books have a home.

> **caution**
> A sagging shelf might quickly develop a permanent curve. When a shelf reaches this state, there's no fix other than to replace the shelf.

Things You'll Need

- ❑ Tape measure
- ❑ Wall-mounted storage system
- ❑ Drill and screwdriver (check shelving instructions for appropriate bit and blade widths)

Using Wall-Mounted Shelves to Stay Organized

There are many types of wall-mounted shelves on the market today, but by far my favorite kind for functionality, looks, and ease of installation are elfa shelves. Elfa is a Swedish company owned by The Container Store. The elfa shelving system is cleverly and simply designed so that anyone can install it with just a few tools. The system is built around a flat horizontal track that attaches to the wall a few inches below the ceiling. After the track is hung, vertical supports (called standards) slide onto the track and brackets for the shelves and accessories snap easily into the standards.

Because the only holes you drill in the wall are the ones at the top to hang the track, the entire shelving system is fully and easily adjustable. You simply lift shelves off the standards, move them, and snap them back into the standards in their new location. Elfa shelves are available in 2', 3', 4', 5', and 6' lengths in either white or platinum and can be custom-cut at no additional charge.

You can also purchase solid shelving in speci-fied fixed lengths of 24" or 30" and depths of 8", 12", 16", or 20". Solid shelving is available in either melamine or wood veneer for a more upscale and attractive look. The system com-ponents are high quality, easy to install, and designed to support 75 pounds per linear foot so they're quite sturdy, even for heavy items such as books.

> **tip**
> When mounting shelves on the wall to be used for books, a shallower shelf is better. Eight to ten inches is generally plenty of depth to accommodate most books. If you'll be stor-ing stacking paper trays, supplies, or larger items, a 12-inch depth would be most effective.

Floating shelves are another kind of wall-mounted shelf you can use for storing or displaying lightweight items in your office. All the mounting hardware is hidden behind the shelf itself so the shelf appears to be floating on the wall. Floating shelves are very popular and they look terrific, offering clean lines and an upscale look in any office (see Figure 11.2).

FIGURE 11.2
Floating wall shelves, such as this mantle shelf from The Container Store, are terrific for displaying art and storing lightweight items in your office. (Photo used with permission.)

You can find floating shelves at The Container Store, as well as other household accessory retailers such as Pottery Barn, Pier One, or Stacks and Stacks (www. stacksandstacks.com). Floating shelves do not hold nearly the amount of weight that a bracket-mounted or an elfa shelf would. Be sure to check the weight specifications of the shelves you purchase so you don't overload them. The last thing you want is to have them come crashing out of the wall, damaging the wall and whatever was sitting on the shelf.

Using Wall Bins, Standing Racks, and Storage Cubes

Shelves aren't the only tool for utilizing vertical space. You also have the option of using wall bins, free-standing racks, and stacking cubes to increase your storage and organization. Wall bins are one of my favorite tools for attaching to open wall space, as well as onto the sides of filing cabinets. You can read all about wall bins and other filing supplies in more detail at the end of Chapter 6.

Standing racks are handy for storing, organizing, and displaying things such as catalogs, product literature, and magazines. They are made of wood, metal, acrylic, or wire and generally take up only about a square foot of floor space. The ones that spin are very efficient because you can store up to four times as much information using all four sides of it rather than having a stationary rack with only one display panel on the front. You can find display racks at any number of online retailers such as OfficeZone (www.officezone.com), Displays2go (www.displays2go.com), and Ergo in Demand (www.ergoindemand.com).

To create a wall of modular storage without using shelves, consider using stacking storage cubes instead. I suspect that the inventor of the stacking storage cube got the idea from his college days when stacked milk crates served as everything from the entertainment center to the dining table!

These handy tools will give you as much storage as traditional shelving and add an interesting design element to your office. Plus they are usually customizable so you can create whatever design you'd like. Cubes are a lot like the toy blocks you played with as a child—you can build them into a square or you can be more creative, choosing to make asymmetric or random shapes.

Stacking cubes can be made from several materials including wood, metal, wire, mesh, or plastic. The type you choose will depend on the look you desire and how sturdy the cubes need to be for the items you're planning to store. If you want to store heavy items, wood or metal is your best bet. If you're creating storage for light-to medium-weight decorative items, any material would be fine as long as you like the way the cubes look. Versatile and fun, storage cubes are a great way to add storage and organization. The Container Store has an unusual galvanized aluminum cube that is very sturdy, quite attractive, and also offers doors and shelves if you want them (see Figure 11.3).

Using Hooks and Door Racks

Hooks are a great way to use the often over-looked space on the back side of a closet or office door. You can hang bags, coats, hats, scarves, or umbrellas in this space, freeing up valuable space elsewhere for office items and supplies. Adhesive hooks are nice because they require no hardware to install, they stick easily to most smooth surfaces, and if you choose Command hooks, you can remove them later without damaging your door. The Command hooks will also

caution If you have hollow doors in your office, be wary of using anything that requires screws for installation. A solid wooden door is strong and accepts wood screws easily. However, a hollow door requires the proper anchor; otherwise, the door is not strong enough to support what you're hanging.

stick onto plaster or drywall and come off without leaving any damage. Be aware that Command and most other adhesive-type hooks will not hold as much weight as a metal or wooden hook that uses screws to install, but they are perfect for light-weight items. You can find Command hooks at The Container Store, Home Depot, Ace Hardware, or almost any other retailer for about $2.50 for a set of two.

FIGURE 11.3
These galvanized aluminum cubes from The Container Store can be configured to make everything from book storage to the base of a desk. (Photo used with permission.)

You can also use the back of almost any door by purchasing a rack specially designed to use the door for storage. Sturdy metal or wooden hooks that use screws to install will hold these racks so you can store CDs, books, videos, office supplies, and much more. Some racks are designed to hang right over the top of the door. These racks come with their own hooks and installation couldn't be simpler. You simply snap the squared metal hook over the top of the door and you're done! You can find over-door racks at The Container Store, Home Depot, Wal-Mart, and several other online retailers such as Organize Everything (www.organizeeverything.com) or Lillian Vernon (www.lillianvernon.com).

Summary

This chapter has given you some good ideas to get you started using the vertical space you might have overlooked in the past. Using wall-mounted shelving for heavier items and floating shelves for art or decorative items is a great way to take advantage of your wall space without sacrificing floor space. Bookshelves are another great option if you do have a little floor space to spare. You can use other tools, such as stacking storage cubes, wall bins, and standing display racks, for additional storage, too. To create even more space, remember to use the back of doors for holding personal items such as hats and jackets, or hang a rack there for keeping office supplies and the like handy but out of the way.

Part V

Appendix

References and Resources

Throughout this book I've made reference to many organizing products as well as suggested places to purchase the products, both online and off. This section will be a helpful guide for you as it groups all the resources by category. I have also added several outstanding resources not mentioned in previous chapters.

Groups and Organizations

This is a list of various groups, companies, and organizations that can help you find a Professional Organizer, learn about getting organized, and deal with related subjects, such as records management and other business services.

American Records Management Association (ARMA)   ARMA is a not-for-profit association and the leading authority on managing records and information, both paper and electronic. Learn more at www.arma.org.

International Association of Administrative Professionals (IAAP)   IAAP provides research on office trends, publications, seminars, conferences, and resources to help administrative professionals enhance their skills and become more effective contributors to their employers. For information, visit www.iaap-hq.org.

National Association of Professional Organizers (NAPO) The first association for the Professional Organizing industry. Founded in 1985, it boasts more than 3,000 members in the United States and across the globe. You can check the website (www.napo.net) to find a Professional Organizer in your area.

National Study Group on Chronic Disorganization (NSGCD) Founded by Judith Kolberg, the NSGCD is open to Professional Organizers and other professionals in the health care and related fields who wish to learn about all aspects of the Chronically Disorganized client. Visit them at www.nsgcd.org.

Product Retailers

Most of these retailers are mentioned within the book, but this section organizes them by product type.

Laptop Bags

Shaun Jackson Design, Inc. Originally a product design house for several well-known consumer brands, Shaun Jackson now creates its own line of unique, patented laptop computer cases that transform into portable work environments (www.shaunjackson.com).

Tom Bihn Tom Bihn himself has been designing and making bags for more than 20 years. His company creates shoulder bags, briefcases, backpacks, and laptop bags (www.tombihn.com).

Filing Supplies and Software

Monticello Corporation Paper Tiger is Kiplinger's electronic file indexing system from Monticello Corporation. Buy the software online (www.thepapertiger.com) or at Office Depot.

Organize Your World Creators of the FileWISE line of filing solutions. FileWISE is available for both home and business use (www.organizeyourworld.com).

Paint

Sherwin-Williams The largest producer of paints and coatings in the United States. Interior and exterior finishes for home and commercial applications (www.sherwin-williams.com).

Organizing Tools, Furniture, and Accessories

The Container Store   Founded in 1978, this privately held company offers unique and beautiful storage and organization solutions for home and office. Superb service and commitment to integrity are among its many strong points. Buy in the store or online (www.containerstore.com).

Franklin Covey   A worldwide leader in effectiveness training, productivity tools, and assessment services for organizations, teams, and individuals (www.franklincovey.com).

Home Depot, Inc.   The world's largest home improvement retailer. It sells items that can be used at home or in the office for storage and organization (www.homedepot.com).

Office Depot, Inc.   Founded in 1986, Office Depot is one of the world's largest sellers of office products. Buy in the store or online (www.officedepot.com).

OfficeMax, Inc.   An office supply store with more than 1,000 retail locations in the United States (www.officemax.com).

Pier One Imports   Casual furnishings and décor for home and office. Pier One's inventory is imported from more than 50 countries (www.pier1.com).

Pottery Barn   A retailer of upscale, comfortable home furnishings and accessories for kids, teens, and adults (www.potterybarn.com).

Space Savers   A specialty retailer offering products to help organize the home and office. Very limited store locations. Buy in the store or online (www.spacesavers.com).

Stacks and Stacks   A California-based company since the mid-1980s, Stacks and Stacks has only one physical location, but offers all its organizing products online (www.stacksandstacks.com).

Staples, Inc.   Founded in 1986 in Brighton, Massachusetts, Staples is the world's leading seller of office products. Buy in the store or online (www.staples.com).

Internet and Mail Order–Only Retailers

Lillian Vernon   A 54-year-old company retailing home and office gadgets, organizing tools, furniture, and accessories exclusively by mail. It specializes in offering many personalized products and has six different catalogs from which to choose (www.lillianvernon.com).

OnlineOrganizing.com   An organizing resource for those interested in becoming a Professional Organizer or those who struggle with disorganization. This popular Internet site (www.onlineorganizing.com) offers free monthly articles, newsletters, and tips, as well as sells a gigantic number of organizing products.

Organize Everything   An online retailer of everything organizational! Searchable Internet site enables you to find just what you need and have it delivered right to your door (www.organizeeverything.com).

Viking Office Products   A retailer of thousands of office supplies and equipment offering no physical retail locations. Products are ordered exclusively by catalog via phone, fax, or Internet (www.viking.com).

Product Manufacturers

Avery Dennison   Labels and other office products (www.avery.com).

Best Software   Makers of ACT! contact management software. ACT! has more than 700 certified consultants worldwide to assist small- and medium-sized businesses with implementation, customization, training, and support (www. bestsoftware.com and www.act.com).

Brother   Maker of faxes, printers, electronic label makers, sewing machines, and other household electronic products (www.brother.com).

Intuit   Makers of tax and financial software (QuickBooks and TurboTax) for business and individual use (www.quickbooks.com).

Pendaflex by Esselte, Corp.   The parent company to Pendaflex and Dymo, Esselte is a leading provider of office and records management equipment, supplies, and products, and home of the "I Hate Filing Club" (www.pendaflex.com).

Restoring Order   A line of high-end office organizing tools for those who love beauty. These contemporary metal accessories include a rubbish bin, drawer dividers, action center, pencil station, and several more (www.restoringorder.com).

Smead   A leading producer of filing and records management products (www.smead.com).

Suggested Reading

ADD Friendly Ways to Organize Your Life, by Judith Kolberg and Kathleen Nadeau, Ph.D. Co-written by the founder of the National Study Group for Chronic Disorganization, this book is loaded with easy, very reasonable strategies to help people with ADD regain control of their lives and work. Recommended for individuals with ADD and those living or working with them. Published by Brunner-Routledge. ISBN 1583913580. Order from www.fileheads.net.

Clear Your Clutter with Feng Shui, by Karen Kingston. The Feng Shui practices are the main focus of this book, but Karen gives a lot of information about clutter; why people create a cluttered, disorganized environment for themselves; and how to change it. Published by Broadway. ISBN 0767903595.

The Complete Communicator, by Bill Lampton, Ph.D. Clear communication is an important part of streamlining your work experience. This upbeat book full of personal stories and anecdotes shows you how communication breaks down and how to improve it, increasing your chances of success. Dr. Lampton offers practical tips for both personal and business situations, including increasing understanding, fostering listening skills, speaking to groups, understanding feedback, and improving writing. Published by Hillsboro Press. ISBN 1577361334.

Organizing from the Inside Out, Second Edition, by Julie Morgenstern. Morgenstern has reworked her original *Organizing from the Inside Out*, which teaches you to organize according to your own personality and style. The second edition includes sections on how to live or work with a disorganized person; how to organize briefcases, handbags, and travel bags; and has included a fully updated resource guide for readers. Published by Owl Books. ISBN 0805075895.

The Seven Habits of Highly Effective People, by Steven Covey. This book was first published in 1990 and still sells like gangbusters because it's packed full of intensely thought-provoking information dealing with personal responsibility, leadership, and self-management. Covey shares compelling information about the qualities and behaviors common to successful people. I consider *The Seven Habits* a must-read for anyone who wants to make the most of their life both personally and professionally. Published by Free Press. ISBN 0671708635.

Taming the Office Tiger, by Barbara Hemphill. A leader in business productivity training, Barbara Hemphill's *Taming the Office Tiger* is a guide to being organized at work. It addresses everything from time management to email, from paper management to how to use a calendar effectively. Published by Kiplinger Books. ISBN 0812927125.

Time Management for the Creative Person, by Lee Silber. This book is terrific for those who tend to be creative, right-brain types struggling with effective use of their time. Silber teaches that the dominant side of a person's brain will tend to influence her habits and behaviors. He offers practical strategies for managing time at home and at work, and becoming more effective and fulfilled as a result. Published by Three Rivers Press. ISBN 0609800906.

Internet Learning Resources and Services

The Internet also offers a wealth of information and services that can help you make a pre-emptive strike against disorganization and the problems it creates.

Stop the Junk

Remove yourself from junk mail and spam email lists by contacting the Direct Marketing Association (www.dmaconsumers.org/cgi/offmailinglist).

Add your phone numbers to the National Do Not Call Registry (www.donotcall.gov/default.aspx).

Opt out of pre-approved credit card offers by calling 1-888-5-OPTOUT (567-8688).

Kim Komando will teach you everything you always wanted to know about keeping your computer system running optimally, avoiding spam and viruses, what is the best free- and shareware, and literally hundreds of other helpful topics. A must for your browser bookmarks (www.komando.com)!

Learn more about the Health Insurance Portability and Accountability Act (HIPAA) if you are in the health or medical field (www.hipaa.org).

Read reviews on consumer electronics such as handhelds, computers, and the like at www.cnet.com.

For articles about all things computers, visit www.pcsupportadvisor.com.

For researching technology questions, visit www.tech-forums.net.

Online Data Backup Services

Backing up data online is an option that many business people use and find simple and convenient. The following list is a few of the companies that offer this service. Prices and rates will vary with each company, so research them before making any decisions to be sure you are choosing the one that is right for your needs.

- EVault (www.evault.com)
- @Backup (www.backup.com)
- Data Protection (www.dataprotection.com)
- Streamload (www.streamload.com)

Antivirus, Antispyware, Antispam, and Firewall Providers

Many companies are offering bundled software to help you combat not only viruses, but also spam, spyware, and hackers, among other threats. The following list is a few of the ones that come highly recommended. Some offer completely free versions for everyone, while others offer free software for home use and charge for commercial use. Each site is different and I recommend you do a little reading on each one before making any decisions. Don't be wary of free products—some of the best software available today is freeware.

- AdAware by Lavasoft (www.lavasoft.de)
- Avast! Antivirus (www.avast.com)
- AVG Anti-Virus from Grisoft (www.grisoft.com)
- Etrust EZ Antivirus from Computer Associates (www.ca.com)
- Kaspersky Labs (www.kasperskylabs.com)

- Spybot Search and Destroy (www.safer-networking.org)
- Trend Micro (www.TrendMicro.com)
- Zone Labs (www.zonelabs.com)

Index

hardwood floors, 55
laminate, 54
mats, 54
rugs, 54-55
tiled, 54
wood, 54
flowers. *See* **plants**
fluorescent lights, 57
focus, maintaining, 70. *See also* **time management**
folders. *See* **file folders**
Franklin Covey, 65, 187
full extension drawers, 103-104
furniture
chairs, 42, 55
choosing, 40
dedicating zones, 40
desks, 41, 47-49
effective office layouts, 40, 46
filing cabinets, choosing, 102
hutches, 41
layouts. *See* office layouts
open filing shelves, 105
positioning, 47
primary furniture, definition of, 40
scale modeling, 43-46
secondary furniture, definition of, 40

G - H

goals, 19-20
"green" flooring
bamboo, 55
cork, 55
definition of, 54
groups. *See* **organizations**

hackers, defeating, 190
halogen lighting, 57
Hand Off bin, 137
hand-written labels
advantages of, 120
for Scarlett O'Hara archetypes, 122
using, 120

hanging accordion folders, 109
hanging file boxes, 109
hanging file folders, 111. *See also* **file folders**
box-bottom folders, 109
choosing to avoid, 105
definition of, 108
EasyView folders, 109
legal size, 108
letter size, 108-109
Oxford Decoflex, 115
ReadyTab folders, 109
specialty products, 109
hanging media files, 110
hanging wall bins, 112-113
hardwood floors, 55
Health Insurance Portability and Accountability Act (HIPAA), 89, 190
home businesses, 21
Home Depot, Inc., 187
hooks, 179
horizontal blinds, 55. *See also* **blinds**
hotels, 168-170
hutches, 41

I

icons (computer), 146-148
identification codes (on files). *See* **filing systems**
identity theft, 25
In Progress file, 134-136
in-boxes, 138
email in-boxes, 153
paperwork in-boxes, 138
indexing systems, 95. *See also* **electronic indexing systems**
indirect access systems. *See* **filing systems**
information
filing. *See* filing systems
sorting, 22-26
information flows, 22. *See also* **workflows**
determining the best flow, 30
increasing effectiveness, 22

interior decorating. *See* **décor**
interior file folders, 111-112
International Association of Administrative Professionals (IAAP), 185
internet retailers, 187-188
interruptions
avoiding, 70
email interruptions, handling, 73
handling, 69
human interruptions, 70-71
phone interruptions, 71-72
Intuit, 188

J - K

junk mail
credit card ads, stopping, 190
sorting, 138
stopping, 189

Kiplinger's electronic indexing system, 95, 98, 186

L

L-shaped desks, 41
labels
computer-printed labels, 121
creating with Microsoft Word, 121
electronic label makers, 122
file labels, 120
hand-written labels, 120
naming files, 124
Pendaflex ReadyTab folders, 120
personal label makers, 122-123
professional labelers, 123
tips for Scarlett O'Hara archetypes, 122

Looking for professional organizing assistance?

Contact the Organizing Authority!

The National Association of Professional Organizers

Whether you need to organize your business or your home, NAPO members are ready to help you meet the challenge.

A professional organizer enhances the lives of clients by designing systems and processes using organizing principles and through transferring organizing skills. A professional organizer also educates the public on organizing solutions and the resulting benefits.

NAPO currently has more than 3,300 members throughout the U.S. and around the world ready to serve you.

For More Information or to Find a Professional Organizer in Your Area,

Visit the NAPO Web Site at **www.NAPO.net**.

Do Even More
...In No Time

Must See

Get ready to cross off those items on your to-do list! *In No Time* helps you tackle the projects that you don't think you have time to finish. With shopping lists and step-by-step instructions, these books get you working toward accomplishing your goals.

Check out these other *In No Time* books, available now!

Organize Your Home In No Time
ISBN: **0-7897-3371-4**
$16.95

Organize Your Work Day In No Time
ISBN: **0-7897-3333-1**
$16.95

Speak Basic Spanish In No Time
ISBN: **0-7897-3223-8**
$16.95

Organize Your Garage In No Time
ISBN: **0-7897-3219-X**
$16.95

Write a Business Plan In No Time
ISBN: **0-7897-3272-2**
$16.95

Organize Your Family's Schedule In No Time
ISBN: **0-7897-3220-3**
$16.95